T0330626

ROUTLEDGE LIBRARY EDITIONS:
ACCOUNTING HISTORY

Volume 6

ALEXANDER HAMILTON CHURCH

ALEXANDER HAMILTON CHURCH
A Man of Ideas for All Seasons

RICHARD VANGERMEERSCH

Routledge
Taylor & Francis Group

LONDON AND NEW YORK

First published in 1988 by Garland Publishing, Inc.

This edition first published in 2021
by Routledge
2 Park Square, Milton Park, Abingdon, Oxon OX14 4RN

and by Routledge
52 Vanderbilt Avenue, New York, NY 10017

Routledge is an imprint of the Taylor & Francis Group, an informa business

British Library Cataloguing in Publication Data
A catalogue record for this book is available from the British Library

ISBN: 978-0-367-33564-9 (Set)
ISBN: 978-1-00-304636-3 (Set) (ebk)
ISBN: 978-0-367-52270-4 (Volume 6) (hbk)
ISBN: 978-1-00-305725-3 (Volume 6) (ebk)

Publisher's Note
The publisher has gone to great lengths to ensure the quality of this reprint but points out that some imperfections in the original copies may be apparent.

Disclaimer
The publisher has made every effort to trace copyright holders and would welcome correspondence from those they have been unable to trace.

Alexander Hamilton Church

A Man of Ideas for All Seasons

RICHARD VANGERMEERSCH

GARLAND PUBLISHING, INC.

NEW YORK & LONDON 1988

For a list of Garland's publications in accounting,
see the final pages of this volume.

Copyright © 1988
by Richard G. J. Vangermeersch

Library of Congress Catalogimg in Publication

■ ■
Vangermeersch, Richard G. J.
Alexander Hamilton Church : a man of ideas for all seasons /
Richard Vangermeersch.
p. cm. — (Foundations of accounting)
Bibliography: p.
Includes index.
ISBN 0-8240-6120-9 (alk. paper)
1. Church, A. Hamilton (Alexander Hamilton), 1866-
2. Managerial accounting. I. Title. II. Series.
HF5635.V243 1988
658.1'511—dc 19   88-17491

Design by Renata Gomes

The volumes in this series are printed on
acid-free, 250-year-life paper.

Printed in the United States of America

PREFACE

My interest in Alexander Hamilton Church started with a project that Henry Schwarzbach and I did on a revision of cost accounting for highly capital-intensive firms. I had purchased Church's 1917 book for 25 cents a few years ago and found it to be a great help in this revision. An article, "Why We Should Account for the Fourth Cost of Manufacturing" published in *Management Accounting* in July, 1983, received a Certificate of Merit from the National Association of Accountants and was given a brief, but eye catching review, in *The Journal of Accountancy* in November, 1983. The review was entitled "Cost Accounting: Does It Need Updating?" and stressed that cost accounting may be 200 years behind the times. We labeled our approach the "machine labor rate approach" and have presented it at numerous robotics seminars at and for The University of Rhode Island Robotics Center. I presented a paper, "Cost Accounting Rethought in the Age of Robotics" at the Robots Nine Conference in Detroit in June of 1985.

I presented a paper "The Wisdom of Alexander Hamilton Church" at the 1983 Annual Meeting of the American Accounting Association. Bob Kaplan utilized this paper in both his keynote address at that convention and in his July, 1984 article in *The Accounting Review* entitled "The Evolution of Management Accounting." He also noted the study on machine labor done by Henry and myself. The paper on A. H. Church was subsequently revised and issued as Working Paper No. 63 by The Academy of Accounting Historians.

As example of the increased interest in Church, I have recently edited a book for Garland Press entitled *The Contributions of Alexander Hamilton Church to Accounting and Management*. This anthology collects many of Church's articles and some related writings on Church's efforts by his contemporaries. I have also written a brief biography of Church, as he was one of the 16 notable accountants in the past chosen for inclusion in a short book done by Random House under the auspices of The Academy of Accounting Historians.

I have included Church as one of the ten writers reviewed in "Milestones in the History of Management Accounting" at the NAA *Cost Accounting for the 90's Conference* in April of 1986.

An article, "The Diagram of the Cost System of Hans Renold Ltd.," was published in the Spring, 1987 issue of *The Accounting Historians Journal*. Tom Johnson and Bob Kaplan in their well received book, *Relevance Lost: The Rise and Fall of Management Accounting*, placed A. H. Church as a key figure in the history of scientific management movement in accounting.

All of this interest indicates a need for an holistic review of Church's efforts in accounting, management, business and society, and industrial engineering. This monograph presents this type of review. I hope the readers gain as much from it, as I did in researching it.

Church spent his last 15 years in the Southern New England area. This fact helped spur me, as I live in nearby Rhode Island. Research was done on Church both in London and in Manchester as a part of a sabbatical year. Two of his former employers were visited in the Manchester area.

I would like to thank Lois Pazienza for her help in tying the many drafts of the text. Frances Harrington did a nice job in editing the final draft. Dick Gauthier and Sharon of the URI Printing Service did a fine job in typesetting the final copy.

September 1, 1987
Kingston, Rhode Island

TABLE OF CONTENTS

LIST OF FIGURES

CHAPTER ONE
INTRODUCTION

Why Should You Read This Monograph About
Alexander Hamilton Church

Categorizing Alexander Hamilton Church into a neat classification is as impossible a task as defining the one ideal reader for this monograph. Clearly, Church aptly fulfills the occasionally abused title of a "man of many ideas." The reader of this monograph, then, must be prepared to shift from discussions on accounting and management to discussions on more general business topics and on industrial engineering. Admittedly, Church preferred to label himself an industrial engineer, whereas it is possible to think of him as a classic forerunner of a management accountant.

It is important to reassess the data on Church because significant gaps and possible misinterpretations exist in the single, brief biography of Church, which appeared in *The Golden Book of Management*. Of all the 70 biographies in the first edition written by Lyndall F. Urwick, Church's biography was the least complete. This writer can sympathize with Urwick, though. It is evident, however, that Church was involved with a number of the early pioneers of management. Joseph Slater Lewis, Hans Renold, and L.P. Alford were well acquainted with Church. Evidently, Church had some dealings with Carl Barth, Dexter S. Kimball, and H.L. Gantt as well. Clearly, Church was greatly influenced by the writings of Harrington Emerson and even more enamored with Charles Babbage, the man Church chose as his major role model. Still, despite this lengthy list of names, much of Church's background is sketchy. The writer found it necessary to go beyond the existing scholarship, such as Paul Garner's *Evolution of Cost Accounting to 1925*, M.C. Wells' *Accounting for Common Costs*, Joseph A. Litterer's "Alexander Hamilton Church and the Development of Modern Management," Mariann Jelinek's "Toward Systematic Management: Alexander Hamilton Church," and Ralph Currier Davis' *The Fundamentals of Top Management*. Two of Church's employers in Great Britain, B. & S. Massey and the Renold Company, were visited by the writer to obtain evidence of the cost systems that Church had installed.

While Church's accounting and management writings have been reviewed in the literature of accounting and management, they have not been treated in an holistic manner, nor have his writings in business and society and in industrial engineering been reviewed. Of course, the fact that Church never compiled his works into a cohesive whole at least partly explains why his works have received such diversified attention. But, as will be demonstrated, some central themes run throughout Church's works, which allow a drawing of parallels between the seemingly diverse fields of engineering and accounting.

Even the comparatively more complete study of Church's efforts in cost accounting deserves a more detailed study, particularly since there is a noticeable resurgence of interest in that topic. The key mover in this resurgence of interest has been Robert S. Kaplan, a former Dean of the Graduate School of Industrial Management at Carnegie-Mellon University and the present holder of the Arthur Lowes Dickenson Chair at Harvard. In an article published in the July, 1984 issue of *The Accounting Review*, Kaplan stated that "... there have been virtually no major innovations by practicing managers or management accountants during the most recent 60 years to affect contemporary management accounting thought." It is possible to recapture the exciting era of industrial accounting during the very late 1800's and the early 1900's, if there is a rediscovery of a more composite potrait of Church and a more composite analysis of the far-reaching effects Church's systems have had upon accounting, management, business and society, and industrial engineering.

The past impact of engineers and engineering concepts on accounting and management have been sorely overlooked. The discussion in this monograph of the impact of Church's engineering background may inspire a much needed dialogue among engineers, accountants, and managers. This dialogue has almost been non-existent for 50 to 60 years.

The previous lack of data on Church carries over to an understatement of the discord between Church and the scientific management school of Frederick Winslow Taylor. Researchers Litterer and Jelinek have hardly exhausted the relationship between Church and the Taylor school. There was a much more open conflict existing between Church and the Taylor School than had been previously argued by those researchers.

But despite stressing the theoretical impact of Church's ideas upon contemporary business structures, this writer does not neglect the very practical implications of Church's work. Church geared his writings toward the working man in industry, not the scholar. In short, Church's writings sprang from his work experiences and, in turn, he strove to better the common man's work day. He was the originator of the scientific machine hour rate and a myriad of equally revolutionary concepts. Consider, for instance, the supplementary rate charged for idle time, the multi-factors of production approach, the concept of production centers, the imputation of interest, and the control of waste—to name just a few.

Church appeals to at least four groups of readers. The first group consists of those readers who are interested in the history of accounting, especially in the cost/managerial area. Unlike most other writings on the history of accounting, therefore, this monograph does not focus on the history of financial accounting. Other readers may be more interested in the history of management, while another group may be more drawn to discussions of Church's efforts in industrial engineering. Finally, some readers may be more receptive to the practical applications of Church's ideas on accounting, management, and engineering systems focused on the world of robotics.

Organization of the Monograph
and Preview of Key Ideas

The second chapter contains an update of Urwick's biography of Church, lists his publications, discusses his relationships with the early pioneers of management, and gives illustrations of Church's character. Chapters 3 and 4 review Church's writings in accounting. Chapter 5 covers his writings in management, while Chapter 6 reviews his writings in the fields of business and society and of industrial engineering. Conclusions are given in the last chapter.

Church was so full of ideas that it is very easy to miss some of them. The writer, therefore, decided to preview 125 ideas from Church in this section. These ideas come from the chronological review of Church's writings first in accounting, followed by his writings in management, in business and society, and in industrial engineering. These ideas are highlighted at the end of the writer's review of each of Church's writings, are categorized in Table 10 in the last chapter, and then selected ones are grouped by central themes in that chapter. The list of the 125 key ideas, hence, follows in the next 13 paragraphs.

(1) Overhead is a product cost. (2) The machine hour rate method is a far superior method of accounting for overhead in a highly capital-intensive firm than other methods of overhead accounting. (3) The production center is the lowest level of collection of accounting data and might be just one machine. (4) The machine should be the focal point of management efforts. (5) Accounting is a vital part of managerial control. (6) All costs should be recorded, allocated to jobs, and be recovered in the selling price. (7) Imputed interest on capital is an overhead cost to the firm. (8) Direct labor approaches to overhead allocation are disastrous. (9) Overhead is growing, while direct labor costs are shrinking. (10) Machines must not be idle. (11) Accounting should immediately highlight idle machines, and, hence, idle capacity.

(12) There are many factors of production. (13) Overhead must be analyzed by factors of production. (14) There should be a comparison of actual costs to standard costs. (15) Overtime must be controlled. (16) Fixed/variable analysis is extremely helpful in controlling overhead. (17) There are principles of overhead treatment. (18) The techniques of applying the principles of overhead are going to vary with the situation at hand. (19) Overhead is the cost of capacity to produce. (20) The cost of capital should be broadly based. (21) The accountant has to be as vitally involved in issues of waste, spoilage, scrap, and by-products as he is in accounting for utilization of machinery. (22) Work being performed in the plant must be controlled by a detailed job and production order system. (23) One must take account of the timing of expenses in passing judgment on management performances for a given time period. (24) The six factors of production are machinery, organization, supervision, stores transport, power, and space.

(25) What happens when the last direct laborer is gone from the plant? (26) All catastrophies and accidental items should be excluded from overhead. (27) Budgeting mandated the service-factor calculations. (28) Standards should be changed whenever any element of direct cost is no longer identical with its corresponding item in the standard cost card. (29) Standards must be checked against actual accounting data. (30) While management must know the profit from each job, they should not disclose this in financial accounting reports because of the many suppositions going into this profit calculation. (31) Revaluations of property for financial accounting purposes should not be given effect in the cost accounting records because of internal comparison purposes. (32) Direct labor might be merged with overhead costs to get a single processing rate. (33) A constant amount of a total of depreciation and interest provides the best figure for cost planning purposes. (34) It is possible to find a rational basis for allocating factors such as storage-transport, supervision, and organization. (35) Management may use the machine-hour rate concept as a "super rate" to analyze its current allocation method and its operating efficiency.

(36) The manufacturing world has entered an extremely more complex arena. (37) The control system for an organization is as needed as and similar in function to the nervous system of a person. (38) The control system must replace the master's eyes and brains in the daily progress of work. (39) The increasing threat of competition has caused the need for complex control systems to coordinate the many parts of the organization. (40) Each business is different, and local needs must be met within the framework of overall principles. (41) Prime costs are not enough to know. (42) The accounting staff should be in a centralized location. (43) A continuous stock-taking system is necessary to arrive at the needed accounting statements. (44) The United States is where to look for progress in manufacturing.

(45) Scientific management is a body of principles and not a system. These principles may be applied in a great variety of ways, as long as the principles are kept. (46) Scientific management has not settled the warring claims of capital and labor. (47) The following of the principles of management will lead to a greater pot to be shared by employees. (48) Labor is not the creator of all wealth. (49) Change should be evolutionary, not revolutionary. (50) The role of the foreman is to provide elasticity of reactions to current events within the rigidity of the organization. (51) The foreman represents the last outpost of general control and is the master's eyes for that department.

(52) The three principles of management are: (1) the systematic use of experience; (2) the economic control of effort; and (3) the promotion of personal effectiveness. (53) The systematic use of experience is the careful analysis of what is about to be attempted and its reference to existing records and standards of performance. (54) A "square deal" is needed for workers. (55) Leadership is probably the most important part of a fine work atmosphere. (56) Good work habits should be created for all.

(57) Management is concerned with "analysis" and "synthesis"—the constructive instrument which builds. (58) "Analysis" focuses on cost accounting, which records and compares the money value of each of the very small steps in the production process. (59) "Synthesis" is the choice, the relative effectiveness, the right proportion, the right kind of means that is in question. (60) The five organic functions of management are design, equipment, control, comparison, and operation. (61) Control fixes the relations of persons throughout the plant and selects the right personalities to fill these posts. (62) The goal of comparison is to substitute quantitative for qualitative measurement methods. (63) Accounting must be concerned with efficiencies measured in time, numbers, and weight, as well as in dollars. (64) Accounting should not be governed by mechanical appliances, in that the work has been fitted to the machine rather than the machine used as an aid to indispensable work. (65) Results of operations must be controlled and safeguarded by a thoroughly modern accounting system. (66) Records of waste must be tied into the general accounting system. (67) A job should be analyzed to determine the special human faculty concerned. (68) Tests should be used to determine the faculties of the job applicants. (69) *Espirit de corps* must be fostered. (70) The technique of time study should best be conducted off the shop floor and be the basis for establishing new and better work habits. (71) Men will manipulate their behavior to give the appearance of doing well. (72) Incentive systems should call out the full use of the talents of that particular grade of worker. (73) The group bonus system can enhance group pride. (74) Workers need to have confidence in the records of the firm in the computation of the group bonus. (75) Time study must take into account the gains in skill in doing a long repeated job. (76) Each kind of equipment must be present in the right proportion and in the right quantity. (77) Each department must be allocated the proportional amount of space fitted to its needs. (78) Expansion to meet new business must be planned. (79) There should be a Book of the Plant. (80) Equipment must be arranged so that product, persons and communications follow the path of best effort. (81) There should be an idle time chart for machinery.

(82) The foreman must have exceptional matters brought to his attention. (83) Immediate recording is needed for immediate discussions to be held. Detail must be piping-hot. The people who make the detail are the people who can use the detail. (84) There should be a master schedule which controls all the sequences of work done. (85) Budget/actual comparisons should be made.

(86) Commercial wastes and by-products must be better marketed. (87) To insure competitiveness, the executive must continually be on the search for new ideas, new machinery, and new methods. (88) Selling costs and office costs are to be analyzed in many different ways, including unit costs. (89) A customer on the books should be a permanent asset to the business. (90) Every complaint must be analyzed by one official or one department. (91) Specialized machines should not be installed unless there is practical assurance that they can be kept working to their full capacity. (92) The executive should seek or accept business for which the plant is perfectly fitted. (93) The product, even machinery, should have a good appearance. (94) The cost of a thing made is a very different matter from the cost of the same thing sold. (95) The selling function must be routinized by use of a sales manual and by a careful layout of sales routes. (96) The sales forecast is crucial. (97) A technical library and information system must be established.

(98) Vagueness of all kinds is one of the great business pitfalls. (99) Meters and recorders, as well as calculating and statistical machines, must be known by the executive. (100) The

amount of liability for outstanding purchase orders must be known by the executive. (101) The executive must balance the three factors of successful purchasing. (102) There should be a purchase-order control board. (103) A card system should be established for each worker. (104) Employee committees lead to better decisions for employee social expenditures than paternalism.

(105) Until some notion of a fair day's work for a fair day's wage comes along, labor strife will continue. (106) Low wages are not necessarily good nor high wages necessarily bad. (107) When a new method of production replaces a worker, the productive capacity of the world increases. (108) All the government measures in the world would not stop trade from flowing to the most efficient countries. (109) Industry cooperation would tend to stabilize production amongst the firms. (110) A market monopoly which did not raise prices is not harmful. (111) Consumer combines can offset monopoly power. (112) Let the democratization of industry evolve. (113) The opportunity to rise out from the rank and file is not a solution to the class problem. (114) Paying men in the same rank more than others threatens group solidarity. (115) Mutual cooperation between management and trade unions must occur before mutual help can replace mutual suspicion.

(116) The decrease in burden per unit is a key factor in adopting a worker incentive method. (117) Unless care is exercised by management, an employee incentive method can lead to much more benefits for the worker than for the firm. (118) When the burden rate is low, the premium should also be at a low rate. (119) The interests of the employee and the employer in a wage incentive system must not conflict. (120) There will be a time when the ultimate efficiency will be known and the piecework controversies will go away.

(121) Numbered spaces and numbered skids must be matched. (122) There is a trade-off between ease of handling and space. (123) Minimum handling cannot be affected in crowded spaces without the employment of specially designed and complex machinery, if possible at all. (124) There should be a large scale plan of the plant with a flow diagram of material movements on the plan. (125) There should be cooperation between architects, construction engineers, and industrial engineers while the plant is being designed.

In addition to highlighting the key ideas for each of Church's writings, comments from other reviewers about Church's efforts are given. The writer also comments about the seven other topics mentioned in the chapter. Was Church a classic forerunner of a management accountant? What are the gaps and possible misinterpretations in Church's background? What were the relationships of Church with the early pioneers of management? Is it possible to give an holistic view of Church's writings? Are there case studies of Church's systems in management accounting? How valuable was engineering input into management and accounting? What was the relationship of the Taylor School to Church?

CHAPTER TWO
WHO WAS ALEXANDER HAMILTON CHURCH

Resume of A. H. Church

Urwick's brief biography of Church was the starting point for a resume of Church, but it is not the final point. Although not having answered all the lingering questions on Church's life and works, the writer has collected enough diverse and new sources to correct past mis-interpretations and to fill-in gaps where there had previously been no information.

Church was born on October 11, 1866[1] near London, England. His parents, however, were American.[2] According to *The Golden Book of Management*, Church "entered the service of the National Telephone Company after a liberal education and later became technical expert and works manager in an electrical manufacturing business."[3] Urwick also noted that Church was probably educated at Oxford.[4] But, contrary to Urwick's assumption, the Registrar at Oxford and several researchers at the Congressional Library told the writer there is no record of Church's enrollment at Oxford.

Urwick wrote that Church worked as an electrical engineer for P.R. Jackson & Co. (Salford, Lancastershire) during the time J. Slater Lewis—a major influence on Church—was working at the same company.[5] Urwick's brief biography of J. Slater Lewis listed 1895 as the date that he started working for P.R. Jackson & Company.[6] Church was then employed at B. & S. Massey in Manchester, "where he reorganized the costing and financial accounting methods used and made improvements in office management."[7] "All I know about his association with B. & S. Massey is memory of conversations I had with my father (Mr. Leonard Massey)," Keppel Massey related to the writer by letter. "When Mr. Leonard took control in the 1890's, costing was on a simple tonnage basis which worked reasonably well as the machines were simple and material was a very large part of the cost and predominantly cast iron. Mr. Joseph Bell, the company's auditor, introduced Mr. Church, who put in the costing system,"[8] which was in effect from about 1900 through 1960.[9] "Mr. Leonard, who was a close friend of Hans Renold, discussed it all with him and Church moved on to Renold's when he completed his assignment with us," explained Mr. Keppel Massey.[10]

Joseph Bell was then an auditor for Parkenson, Mather & Co., an accounting firm very much involved with the manufacturing engineering companies in Manchester at the time.[11] He was regarded as one of the early stalwarts of the Manchester Society of Chartered Accountants.[12]

As reported by Urwick, Church was with Hans Renold in Manchester for five years from 1900 to 1905.[13] Another source had Church's stay with Renold as only three years.[14] Church introduced there his own costing methods.[15] The writer found no specific reference to Church in the substantial archives at the Renold Company, but did uncover some interesting documents in which Church undoubtedly played a part. One of these documents is shown in Chapter 3.

Apparently, Urwick was incorrect when he wrote that in 1905 Church had already transferred his chief activities to the United States.[16] Perhaps, Urwick placed too much emphasis on a 1906 letter sent to the editor of the *American Machinist*. Even though the letter, entitled "Cost and Time-Keeping Outfit of the Taylor System,"[17] was signed with the initials "F.A.H.[18], Urwick contends that Church wrote the article and was, therefore, in America at the time.

It is more likely that Church came to the United States in 1909.[19] Two sources listed Church as either the editor[20] or the manager of the European Edition of *The Engineering Magazine*[21] during some of the years Urwick claims that Church was in America. One of those two sources suggests that Church held the editorial position for seven years.[22] If this is true, there may have been an overlap of two years with the Renold job, or Church may have left Renold in 1902.[23] Unfortunately, a review of *The Engineering Magazine* from 1902 through 1909 did not yield a verification of Church's affiliation with the publication as there were no editorial listings. There were a number of editorial comments, however, that one might attribute to Church. But such conjecture is admittedly pure speculation.

The Engineering Magazine was a hot-bed for works in cost-keeping, wage systems, and general management.[24] Church certainly would have gained a very wide exposure in accounting, management, business and society, and industrial engineering during his stay at *The Engineering Magazine's* London office.[25] Founded by John R. Dunlap in 1891, the publication set the goal of having all engineers, manufacturers, and all industrial managers realize "that they are of necessity economists—and that they must now study industrial economy as a practical science, because it is the very basis of all successful industrial administration."[26] *The Engineering Magazine* then "was the pioneer in industrial management journalism and under Mr. Dunlap's direction over a thirty-seven year period ... rendered a valuable service to industrial progress throughout the world; it became widely noted for its technical discussions of industrial management problems."[27] Dunlap adopted a policy of republishing in book form the serial articles that were in widespread demand.[28]

M.C. Wells observed that Church used the pseudonym of H.C. Alexander in 1909, when he published his six part series on "Organization of Production Factors" in *The Engineering Magazine*.[29] Still, when Wells wrote *A Bibliography of Cost Accounting*, he cited these articles as the work of H.C. Alexander.[30] An examination of the New York edition of *The Engineering Magazine* showed A. Hamilton Church as the author. The writer wrote to Wells and posited that Church may have preferred to use a pseudonym in the London Edition, since he was the London Editor. Wells kindly responded by sending photocopies of the relevant pages from the London Edition where the author byline of H.C. Alexander was plainly visible. Hence, the mystery of the pseudonym remains unsolved but, at least, a possible explanation has been given.

By 1911 Church referred to himself as a "Consulting Expert on Factory Administration with C.H. Scovell & Co., Boston, Mass."[31] According to its ad in the 1913 Boston City Directory, Scovell & Co. was very involved with cost and systems work. Later that same year, Church dropped C.H. Scovell & Co., from his title[32] and, by 1912, was listed as a consulting engineer on 30 Broad St., New York.[33] Church was then employed by Patterson, Teele & Dennis as a consulting industrial engineer.[34] Like his previous place of employment, this firm was also very involved in cost and systems work—as can be seen based on the content of the ad on the following page (See Figure 1) also taken from the 1913 Boston City Directory. Urwick lists Church as an employee of this last firm between the years of 1912 to 1915[35], but this period is most likely too long. To complicate matters further, it is unclear if Church worked in the Boston or New York office of that firm.[36]

It is known, however, that is 1915 Church referred to himself as a "Consulting Industrial Engineer in New York, N.Y., USA.[37]" and that his company was involved in a long term consulting job at the Winchester Repeating Arms Company in 1916 and/or 1917.[38] By the early

Figure 1
Accounting Ads in 1913

Accountants

Clinton H. Scovell & Company

Certified Public Accountants
Industrial Engineers

Constructive Accounting-Audits-Investigations

Costs-Industrial Engineering

110 STATE STREET, BOSTON

PATTERSON, TEELE AND DENNIS

Accountants and Auditors

Specialties; Installation of Cost Systems and Investigations

NEW YORK AND BOSTON

131 STATE STREET   **BOSTON**

Resident Partner, F. S. C. STEELE   Chartered Accountant and Certified Public Accountant

Source: *The Boston City Directory, 1913,* p. 2661 and p. 2666.

9

1920's, Church was a consultant at Mount Hope Finishing in North Dighton, Mass.[39] L.P. Alford, editor of *Management Engineering* at this time, described Church as being engaged in the practice of industrial engineering in this country with "... such varied industries as the manufacture of steel, electric specialities, soap, shoes, ordnance, textiles, and others."[40] As noted later in this chapter, Alford and Church were in close contact and Alford certainly would have known Church's occupation. On the other hand, since Urwick was not on intimate terms with Church, one can understand why Urwick would mistakenly state that Church was a consultant to the Mount Hope Finishing Company in the late 1920's or early 1930's.[41]

When the Mount Hope Finishing Company moved to North Carolina in 1951, it did not take its records from the Church era.[42] But besides Alford's records that title Church as one involved in industrial engineering consulting, Church titled himself as a Consulting Industrial Engineering in 1922,[43] in 1927,[44] in 1931,[45] and in 1934.[46] Specifically the 1927 source listed the following: "Mr. A. Hamilton Church, consulting Industrial Engineer, has been closely connected with the modern industrial engineering movement for the past twenty-five years, during which time he has served a variety of industries—foundry, engineering, soap-making, light manufacturing, guns and shells, shoe-manufacturing, textile-finishing, etc."[47]

Church died in Taunton, Massachusetts on February 11, 1936. While death certificates are not known for their warmth, Church's was particularly cold. (See Figure 2). His burial costs were paid by his last employer, the Mount Hope Finishing Company.[48] His funeral service, held at the Dagen Funeral Home, was conducted by the Reverend Henry Medry of St. Thomas Church in Taunton—a parish in which Church wasn't even a member, according to its current pastor.[49] Church was also not a registered voter in Taunton.[50] And, he was almost a pauper when he died. Church's probate records showed that he died intestate, with no heirs, and assets of just $224.88.[51] Miscellaneous liabilities totaled $25.99; probate costs were $18.24; the probate fee was $50.00; the remainder of $130.65 went to Church's landlady, Mrs. Frederick W. Wood, for care, nursing, and rent.[52]

Clearly, Church had a varied career. As already pointed out, certain facets of it have been inaccurately recorded in Urwick's biography. One of the most significant oversights on Urwick's part was the absence of information on Church's experience as the European editor of *The Engineering Magazine*, an experience that laid a strong groundwork for both his varied interests and writing abilities. Church also published many articles in the magazine. Its emphasis on practical and technical articles meant that, like the other contributors to the magazine, Church conveyed a "hands-on" approach. Church's writings had to be workable, or at least, been tried in practice. A further exploration of this portion of Church's career including his relationship with Dunlap would have been done but, unfortunately, time and mergers have destroyed almost all hope of a more successful exploration of the records of *The Engineering Magazine*.

Church's List of Publication

A new, lengthly list of Church's publications can be found in the Appendix to this Chapter. This list is presented in chronological order and is much lengthier than Urwick's list, whose items are marked by an *. The list in the Appendix exceeds Urwick's and exceeds the listings found in *The Accountant's Index* and the *Readers Guide to Periodical Literature*, because the writer sought out other sources. For example, the 1915 publications were found only by a search through the *American Machinist*, as *The Engineering Index*, from 1913 through 1916 did not index articles form the *American Machinist*.[53] *The Engineering Index* was difficult to use since it did not have an author's index until 1928.[54]

A further discussion of Church's publications will be taken up in the remaining chapters. The discussion and the list in the Appendix have been classified into four areas—accounting, management, business and society, and industrial engineering.

Figure 2
Death Certificate of A. H. Church

Commonwealth of Massachusetts
U. S. A.
City of Taunton

MARY C. GORDON,
ASST. CITY CLERK

I, the subscriber, do hereby certify that it appears by the Register of Deaths of said
Taunton that Alexander Hamilton Church died in Taunton, Massachusetts on
the Eleventh day of February A.D., nineteen hundred and thirty-six.

(February 11, 1936)

The record is in words and figures following, to wit:

No. 120   Date of Death February 11, 1936

Name of Deceased { Alexander Hamilton Church

Sex, Male   Color other than white, —   Condition Single

Age, 75?   years, —   months, — — days.

Disease or cause of death, Primary, Coronary Occlusion,

Contributory, Arterio-sclerosis,

1. *Residence,* 24 Union St., Taunton, Mass.

2. *Place of Death,* 24 Union St., Taunton, Mass.

Place of Burial, Dighton, Massachusetts

Occupation, Retired Consulting Engineer

Place of Birth, England?

Name and Birthplace of father, —— Church, Unknown

Maiden Name and Birthplace of mother, Unknown, Unknown

Name of Cemetery, Unitarian Church

Date of Record, February 14, 1936

Book 17 , *Page* 157

I, Mary C. Gordon *depose and say, that I hold the office of*
CITY CLERK OF THE CITY OF TAUNTON, *County of Bristol and Commonwealth of*
Massachusetts; that the records of Births, Marriages and Deaths of said City are in
my custody, and that the above is a true extract from the Records of Deaths of said
City, as certified by me.

Witness my hand and seal of said City, on the Second

day of November 19 82 .

City Clerk.

11

Relationship with Some Others in *The Golden Bank of Management*

Joseph Slater Lewis' celebrated book, *The Commercial Organization of Factories* (1896), contains in its preface an acknowledgement to A.H. Church for his assistance during various stages of the work.[55] It can be inferred from this reference that Church did not have a university degree. In the preface, Lewis includes a "B.A." after the name of another acknowledged person; Church, on the other hand, has no distinction of degree after his name.[56] Nevertheless, Church was involved in a publication that Urwick considered to be "the earliest comprehensive analysis published in Great Britain, of the fundamentals of industrial administration with special reference to the control function."[57] Like Church, Lewis strove to tie together engineering and accounting.

> ...It is beyond question, however, that the largest and most successful industrial undertakings are those where minuteness of detail and perfection of organization have received paramount consideration: a fact which should, in itself, especially in these days of worldwide competition, make the Commercial Organization of Factories a matter of the first importance in every country with any manufacturing pretensions.
>
> The system of accounts presented in this book is the result of many years' close observation and practical experience, and is, what may be termed, an interlocking system, under which each and every account in an Engineering Factory is brought into line monthly, and a general balance of the whole effected...[58]

Significantly, Church was considered to be the carrier of Lewis' mantle when he died in 1901,[59] just after concluding a series of articles in *The Engineering Magazine* in May, 1900.[60] The last article was delayed because of Lewis' much regretted health[61], but was followed by Church with a December, 1900 article, "The Meaning of Commercial Organization." The following introductory footnote to that article clearly spells out Church's prominence as a leader of the science of management in his own right:

> Mr. Church, the associate of Mr. J. Slater Lewis, is one of the leaders of the new science of modern manufacturing. The strong feature of his article is his demonstration that organization is an integral and even basal part of successful works management—not merely an auxiliary to it—The Editors.[62]

A little over ten years later, another reference to Church's work with Lewis was made in *The Engineering Magazine:*

> During the time while Mr. Gantt was introducing the task and bonus system at the Midvale Steel Works, and even earlier than that; while the historic work of Mr. F.W. Taylor was being carried on at Bethlehem, Mr. Church was associated with J. Slater Lewis in his pioneer undertakings to reduce the commercial organization of factories to the form of practical science. For more than twenty years Mr. Church has been closely associated either with the making or recording of the science of management. His conception of it, therefore, rests upon the ground of intimate knowledge and has the broad perspective given by familiarity with many divisions of the field...[63]

Urwick credits Hans Renold with pioneering a practical experiment in British scientific management in his manufacturing engineering firm.[64] Urwick writes that: "The Renold system of carefully conceived monthly cost-control returns was particularly interesting. These returns covered not only financial matters but also manufacturing activities and stocks. The system had been developed by Renold with the aid of the costing expert A.H. Church, and it became the foundation of modern scientific costing in Great Britain."[65]

The dynamic working relationship between Church and Renold seems to have created an exciting climate for ideas. Notably, though, it was Renold who was most proud of the fact that he had met with F.W. Taylor three times.[66] Three of the early presidents of the Institute of Cost and Work Accountants--Roland Dunkerley, William Walker, and Percy Lightbody--were Renold's employees at about and shortly after the period Church was employed by

Renold.[67] According to Percy Lightbody's obituary, both Renold and Church helped foster the innovative outlook Lightbody possessed:

> Few of us can remember him working with Hamilton Church for Hans Renold, but from both Church and Renold he must have gained an almost unique experience, which he undoubtedly passed on to his colleagues Roland Dunkerley and Willie Walker.
>
> In those days, the firm of Renold was many years in advance of practically every other firm in the country, not only in methods of manufacture but also in management techniques and in budgeting and costing.[68]

Finally, this quote, made by Roland Dunkerley, the recipient of the first Gold Medal of the Institute of Cost and Management (Works) Accountants[69], emphasizes that Church during his Renold period formulated what is perhaps the major cornerstone of his career, the machine hour rate method.

> The advent of machinery of new types, and particularly that of automatic machinery, necessitated a complete revision of the ideas of omnibus expense allocation as being applicable, or even in the slightest degree satisfactory. Accounting problems began to have a different perspective, and sectional and departmental analysis of expenses was adopted in an effort to maintain the percentage on wages method of recovering expenses.
>
> It became increasingly clear that expenses allied to the machine itself needed to be provided for, and that these expenses varied with the running times of the machine; this was ultimately resolved by the provision of what is known as the MACHINE HOUR RATE.
>
> It can therefore be said that modern ideas on costing only date back to the beginning of the present century and to the work of Arthur Hamilton Church, who probably did more than anyone, both directly and indirectly, to promote costing as it is now known, chiefly because he promoted thought. Many of his statements and teachings have been found impracticable in the light of subsequent investigations, but this should not be allowed to detract from the value of his pioneer work.
>
> Church was responsible for devising the machine hour rate as a unit of Works expense distribution, with a supplementary rate on a percentage basis to absorb the total Works expense in costs, and by his G.E.C. (General Establishment Charges), to cover the cost of administration, selling, etc.[70]

Church's involvement with Leon Pratt Alford was by far the most longstanding of the pioneers from *The Golden Book of Management*. An engineer, Alford was the pioneer of management handbooks and was very active in contributing input on management topics for The American Society of Mechanical Engineers (ASME).[71] In addition, Alford became an editor of the *American Machinist* in 1907, rising to the title of Editor in Chief in 1911—a position he retained until 1917.[72] During that time, Church published in the *American Machinist*. Not surprisingly, therefore, when Alford edited the first *Cost and Production Handbook* in 1934, Church was listed as a contributor.[73]

But the most important collaboration of Church and Alford was certainly the widely renowned article, "The Principles of Management," which served as the basis for the 1912 Report of the ASME Subcommittee on Administration, where Alford was the committee secretary.[74] More recently, the article was selected for inclusion in *Classics of Management* by Harwood F. Merrill for the American Management Association.[75] Merrill's introduction highlights that Church and Alford went beyond Taylor's discussion of scientific management by making a semantic distinction on Taylor's definition of "principle."

> THE STATEMENT of *The Principles of Management* which follows this introduction carries with it some of the air of controversy surrounding the subject in the first dozen years of this century. Frederick W. Taylor was deep in his crusade for the principles of scientific management. But many opposed his concepts, and others denied that any principles were even involved in his philosophy.
>
> Alexander Hamilton Church and Leon Pratt Alford, co-authors, were in the latter group. They believed that Taylor was talking, not about principles, but about "a collection of axioms and an arbitrary combination of specific mechanisms" such as time study, task and bonus, and functional foremanship. They wanted to go deeper, and in the effort they came

up with the proposition which follows. Their comments on the frequent lack of relationship between physical working conditions and morale provide a foretaste of Mayo's conclusions.[76]

Carl Barth, another renowned management engineer and "the earliest, ablest, and closest associate of Taylor,"[77] also knew Church. Barth and Church had an exchange of views at the 1912 ASME National Meeting.[78] They had an association at the Winchester Repeating Arms Company, because Barth worked there when Church was a consultant to the firm from about 1916 to 1918.[79] In his article in honor Ralph C. Davis, a leading writer in management during the 1930's to the 1950's, John Mee wrote that during the process of installing a production control system at Winchester, Davis "was able to observe Carl Barth revise the machine speeds and feeds and Dwight Merrick improve the time study practices. Al Currier, from the staff of A. Hamilton Church, provided the consulting function for the production control system."[80] Dexter S. Kimball, who offered the first elective course in works administration at Cornell in 1904 and wrote a text which had a healthy life span of forty years,[81] was quite generous in his praise of Church.[82]

Church also had some lively exchanges with H.L. Gantt. He was famous first for his task and bonus system of wages, secondly for his graphic charts for production control, and thirdly for employer/employee relations.[83] The set of exchanges between Church and Gantt in 1915 is especially interesting.[84] Church frequently praised Harrington Emerson's work on standard costing. He was the originator of, and one of the few genuinely qualified in, the field of "efficiency engineering."[85] Emerson gave tremendous publicity to "scientific management" when he stated, under oath, at an Interstate Commerce Commission hearing "that the railroad companies could save 'a million dollars a day' on their operating costs."[86]

Church was even more impressed with Charles Babbage, who Church considered to be the major forerunner of modern management in a machinery environment. In fact, Church began his 1908 book with two references from Babbage[87] and later credited him with founding the management technique of time study.[88] Babbage's book, *On the Economy of Machinery and Manufacturers*, published in 1832, and his other writings, were the forerunners for such topics as general managerial principles, analysis of manufacturing processes and costs, time study, and comparative management studies.[89]

The relationship between Church and Frederick Winslow Taylor, the world-wide acclaimed "Father of Scientific Management[90], was probably the most intriguing of the aforementioned pioneers of management. Church used Taylor and his disciples as strawmen in order to promulgate his own ideas.[91] Urwick wrote that while Taylor may have stressed the mechanical side of management over its dynamic side, he was not, as Church implied about Taylor's disciples, oblivious to the dynamic side.[92]

> ...His own life and writing, however, provide ample evidence of the integrity and essential rightness of his personal attitude toward those who worked with him and his concept of the obligations of management to society as a whole. There was never a strike in any plant where he personally was operating. It was in accord with his whole outlook that his immediate followers, particularly Gantt and Gilbreth, made a larger contribution to the dynamics of management.[93]

Church and Taylor were present and spoke during the discussion of the 1912 Report of the ASME Subcommittee on Administration,[94] at which discussion Barth was critical of Church's views, as already mentioned. Apparently, Taylor never publicly exchanged views with Church.

The last two pioneers of management had works that Church used as references. James Rowan was very involved in work incentives methods and founded the Rowan method. "It consisted of a fixed time allowance on each job at an hourly rate for that job. A job-data book was built up from which future hourly rates could be determined. The premium paid to the worker was calculated by adding to the hourly wage the same percentage as that by which he had reduced the time allowed for each job..."[95] Frederick Halsey was an American engineer, whose wage incentive work was considered by Urwick to have been the model for the Rowan method.[96]

In summary, Church was certainly involved with some very exciting and renowned individuals during what was indeed an exciting time for the new field of industrial management. More importantly, though, Church ranked with the best of them.

The Character of A.H. Church

One cannot be too definitive when discussing Church's character because he died more than fifty years ago without leaving a trace of family. Even though Urwick admitted that the facts of Church's life and work were hidden in obscurity,[97] he did make some definite statements about Church's character. Urwick concludes his biography of Church with these rather moving paragraphs:

> Church was an exceptionally timid and lonely man. Though he was an authority on accounting and on management, he never joined any of the recognized accounting societies, the Taylor Society, ASME, or any other engineering society. He refused all invitations to speak in public, for he lacked the courage to face a group of people. Yet those few who knew him say he was an unusually charming man, one with whom it was a pleasure to work; that he had gifts, not shared by all the early "efficiency experts," for drawing out useful contributions from those with whom he worked and for finding compromise solutions which won general satisfaction. He was a perfectionist in work, almost an artist, yet he could not bear daily routine. Sometimes he would vanish for weeks at a time and then reappear with a new, constructive idea.
>
> Church never married. Gradually, as he grew older, he became more and more reclusive. It was rumored that he had wealthy relatives, but there is no indication that he ever saw them, or they him. He died alone, with no obituary notices in either the local or the metropolitan journals. Yet his contribtuion to management was as great or greater than that of many whose names are famous in the movement. This shy, solitary, and forgotten man takes a place in *The Golden Book of Management* that he doubly earned.[98]

But three recorded events cast doubt on Urwick's assertion that Church "refused all invitations to speak in public, for he lacked the courage to face a group of people."[99] Church gave at least two papers at professional conferences in the United States. He presented a paper on the "Distribution of Expense Burden" to the spring meeting of the National Tool Builders Association in Atlantic City on May 18 and 19, 1911. F.W. Taylor also gave a talk at that convention but there was no discussion of his talk because of lack of time, leading one to believe that there was a discussion after Church's talk.[100]

Church also spoke at the New York meeting of ASME in 1912 to discuss the report of its Subcommittee on Administration, "The Present State of the Art of Industrial Management." The list of speakers at the discussion was a litany of famous names.[101]

Church also presented a paper at the 1915 International Engineering Congress in San Francisco during the Pan American Exposition.[102] There was a short discussion at the end of that presentation, in which he differentiated between phrenology and applied psychology.[103]

Church apparently was not very gregarious but he also was not unwilling to stand and face controversy, as suggested by Urwick. He appeared quite active in personal exchanges in the decade of 1910, perhaps his key decade.

15

Year

1900 "The Meaning of Commercial Organization," *The Engineering Magazine*, Vol. 20, No. 3, December, pp. 391-398 * MAN.

1901 "British Industrial Welfare," New York: *Cassier's Magazine*, Vol. 19, pp. 404-405. * BUS & SOC

"The Proper Distribution of Establishment Charges," *The Engineering Magazine*, Vol. 21 and 22 (articles in six issues). * ACC

1908 *The Proper Distribution of Expense Burden*, Works Management Library, London: The Engineering Magazine. 116 pages. ACC

1909 "Organization by Production Factors," *The Engineering Magazine*, Vol. 38 (in 6 parts) * ACC

1910 *Production Factors in Cost Accounting and Works Management*, Industrial Management Library, New York: The Engineering Magazine Co., 187 pages ACC

1911 "Distribution of the Expense Burden," *American Machinist*, Vol. 34, Part 2, pp. 991-992, 999 * ACC

"Distribution of the Expense Burden," *The Iron Age*, June 1, pp. 1325-1326. ACC

"Has 'Scientific Management' Science?," *American Machinist*, Vol. 35, pp. 108-112. * MAN

"Intensive Production and the Foreman," *American Machinist*, Vol. 34, Part 2, pp. 830-831 * MAN

"The Meaning of Scientific Management," The Engineering Magazine, Vol. 41, pp. 97-101 * MAN

1912 "The Principles of Management," (with L.P. Alford), *American Machinist*, Vol. 36, pp. 857-861 * MAN

"Direct and Indirect Costs," *American Machinist*, Vol. 36, Jan.-July, p. 763 ACC

The Proper Distribution of Expense Burden, 2nd Edition, New York: The Engineering Magazine Co., 144 pages. ACC

1913 "Comments" on "The Present State of the Art of Industrial Management," Report of Subcommittee on Administration, *Transactions of ASME, 1912*, New York: ASME, 1913, pp. 1156-1159. MAN

"Practical Principles of Rational Management," *The Engineering Magazine*, Volumes 44 and 45 (3 parts in each volume) * MAN

"Premium, Piece Work, and the Expense Burden," *The Engineering Magazine*, October, pp. 7-18. * IND ENG

"Bonus Systems and the Expense Burden," *The Engineering Magazine*, November, pp. 207-216 * IND ENG

"On the Inclusion of Interest in Manufacturing Costs," *The Journal of Accountancy*, April, pp. 236-240. ACC

1914 *The Science and Practice of Management*, New York: The Engineering Magazine Co., 535 pages. * MAN

"The Scientific Basis of Manufacturing Management," *Efficiency Society Journal*, Vol. 3, February, pp. 8-15. * MAN

"What are the Principles of Management?" *Efficiency Society Journal*, Vol. 3, February, pp. 16-18. * MAN

1915   "The Evolution of Design," *American Machinist*, Vol. 42, No. 23, June 20, p. 1008. IND ENG

"Machine Design and the Design of Systems," *American Machinist*, Vol. 43, No. 2, July 8, pp. 61-62. IND ENG

"Mr. Gantt's Theory of Expense Burden," *American Machinist*, Vol. 43, No. 5, July 29, pp. 209-210. ACC

"Relation Between Production and Cost," *American Machinist*, Sept. 2, Vol. 43, No. 10, Sept. 2, 1915. ACC

"What is a Cost System?", *American Machinist*, Vol. 43, No. 11, Sept. 9, pp. 455-457. MAN

"What a Foreman Should Know about Costs," *American Machinist*, Vol. 43, No. 13, Sept. 23, pp. 553-556. MAN

"What the Superintendent Should Know," *American Machinist*, Vol. 43, No. 16, Oct. 14, pp. 675-678. MAN

"What the Executive Wants to Know About Costs," *American Machinist*, Vol. 43, No. 18, October 28, pp. 763-766. MAN

1916   "Industrial Management," *Transactions of the International Engineering Congress, San Francisco, 1915*, pp. 446-472. * MAN

1917   *Manufacturing Costs and Accounts*, New York: McGraw-Hill. 452 pages. * ACC

"The Future of Industry," *The Unpopular Review*, June, pp. 251-272. * BUS & SOC

1922   "Internal Transportation in a Large Textile Finishing Plant-I," *Management Engineering*, Vol. II, Number 4, April, pp. 197-202. IND ENG

"Internal Transportation in a Large Textile Finishing Plant-II," *Management Engineering*, Vol. II, Number 4, May, pp. 293-296. IND ENG

1923   *The Making of an Executive*, New York: D. Appleton & Co., 457 pages. * MAN

1927   "Selecting a Plant Transport System," *Industrial Management*, Dec., Vol. LXXIV, No. 6, pp. 368-371. IND ENG

1929   *Manufacturing Costs and Accounts*, 2nd edition, New York: McGraw-Hill, 507 pages. ACC

1930   *Overhead Expenses in Relation to Costs, Sales, and Profits*, New York: McGraw-Hill, 516 pages. * ACC

1931   "Overhead—The Cost of Production Preparedness," *Factory and Industrial Management*, Jan., pp. 38-41. ACC

1934   "Manufacturing or Production Orders," and "Machine-Hour Rate," *Cost and Production Handbook*, L.P. Alford, Editor, New York: The Ronald Press, pp. 242-245 and pp. 1085-1086, respectively. (These works were attributed to Church by this writer.) ACC

CHAPTER THREE
ACCOUNTING WRITINGS (PART ONE)

The following presentation of Church's accounting writings adopts the same chronological order shown in the List of Publications in Chapter 2. Excerpts and paraphrases from Church's writings are first given for each grouping, followed by comments from other reviewers, and then by comments from this writer. Specifically, the chronological divisions in this chapter are: 1. 1901/1908/1912 (book), 2. 1909/1910, and 3. 1911, 1912 (article) and 1913.

1901/1908/1912(Book)

In essence, the 1912 "revised version" of *The Proper Distribution of Expense Burden* is no different from the original 1908 edition. There were minor format changes, such as one fewer line per page and a slightly larger type—which is why the 1912 book was 144 pages, compared to the 116 pages of the 1908 book. But the actual copy of both books is the same, word-for-word. Furthermore, the 1908 book contains a revised version of Church's 1901 articles in *The Engineering Magazine*. Consequently, these articles are not reviewed separately.

In the 1908 text, Church expressed his philosophy towards management and accounting in what might best be described as the "Parable of the Machine Tool."

> It is true that the broad results of a half-year's work can be read in unmistakable figures in the balance sheet. But the mischief is not only done by that time, but in the absence of proper shop accounts, it cannot be ascertained where is the element at fault. To introduce reform one must first know where reform is necessary. It is no answer to this to say that practical experience supplies the deficiency. A man with a file and a true plane surface can supply a duplicate of that plane surface if he has sufficient skill and works long enough, but he will produce the same result more quickly and surely if he has a machine tool of the highest class to aid him. And in proportion to the accuracy of the machine tool so will be the ease and speed of the performance. A modern system of organization is a high class machine tool. It can be done without, but not economically. That is all there is to it. The wise man will make his own choice.[1]

Church's succinct and matter-of-fact style carried over to his overall philosophy on the correct application of manufacturing overhead. Throughout his writings, he remained extremely concerned about an application of a constant percent of overhead for each job.

> ...Now, a moment's consideration will suffice to show that any system of general percentage must be most unfair. So must the method of basing valuation on simple prime cost. The reason is obvious. All valuation is an attempt to represent certain facts. The facts are indubitably these: the charges incident on a variety of articles as truly represent part of the cost of such articles as the actual direct wages paid on them. And these charges are

rarely, it would be safe to say never, identical in their incidence on different classes of articles nor are they constant from period to period.

Therefore an attempt to represent their value either by ignoring this factor of production or by applying an arbitrary increment or percentage equally on all, will produce not any approach to facts, but merely a fancy figure, which will be not even constant in its error. It is, in fact, a guess, and not the less so because based on figures. Arrangements of this kind probably originated the unkind saying that figures will prove anything, "except facts."[2]

Church was quite concerned with the total cost of a job. He thought it essential that there be an aggregation of profits in each sales item.[3] To clarify the process, Church employed this chart over and over again.[4] (See Figure 3).

FIGURE 3

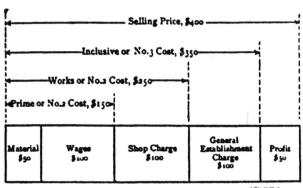

ANALYSIS OF THE SALE PRICE OF A MANUFACTURED ARTICLE.

To further aid the reader in visualizing the problem of applying a constant percent for overhead, Church provided the reader with this illustration.

We find that as against $100 direct wages on order, we have an indirect expenditure of $59, or in other terms, our shop establishment charges are 59 percent of direct wages in that shop for the period in question. This is, of course, very simple. It is also as usually worked very inexact. It is true that as regards to the output of the shop as a whole a fair idea is obtained of the general cost of the work—That is, of its works cost. And in the case of a shop with machines all of a size and kind, performing practically identical operations by means of a fairly average wages rate, it is not alarmingly incorrect.

If, however, we apply this method to a shop in which large and small machines, highly paid and cheap labor, heavy castings and small parts, are all in operation together, then the result, unless measures are taken to supplement it, is no longer trustworthy.[5]

Church's concern about the accounting for manufacturing overhead magnified as the amount of overhead increased in relation to wages of direct laborers. He felt that the amount of manufacturing overhead had reached the point of significance for control purposes.

...These shop charges frequently amount to 100 percent, 125 percent, and even much more of the direct wages. It is therefore often actually more important that they should be correct than that the actual wages cost should be correct. If we have to put a dime and also a quarter in a certain collecting bag, it is certainly more important that the quarter should not go astray than that the dime should be looked after.[6]

Church considered manufacturing overhead to be a series of very specific items, not one general amount. The following passage is preparation for his later and more detailed development of the multi-factors approach to accounting for manufacturing overhead.

...Having entirely cleared one's mind of any traditions of what is usual or conventional under the averaging regime, it becomes visible that several of the items of shop charge are naturally connected with the use and employment of property or plant, and are in the nature of a rent paid for these. In this category are:—Rent, taxes, and insurance on buildings, interest, depreciation on machines, on cranes, shafts, motors, etc. Other items are connected with other factors of production. Power, with the use of same by machines; cost of lighting or heating, with area of floor space usually lighted or heated—in short, not to go into detail at this stage, it is readily seen that a large number of shop charges are by no means general in their real nature but can be narrowed down to definite points of incidence.[7]

A significant part of Church's designing of an approach to account for manufacturing overhead was a proposal for cost collection by production centers.

...But if we regard the shop as a collection of small "production centers," each differing from the other, with certain common connecting bonds which are alone the average or general factors of incidence, then the problem suddenly becomes clear. If instead of turning our energies to cover up the natural differences between these "production centers" and make an average of them, we devote our attention to giving the fullest plan to this difference, we may claim to have subdivided the shop in a new sense, and to a new end.[8]

When Church proceeded with the little shop analogy to illustrate the production center basis, he again was careful to contrast this approach to the averaging approach.

A production center is, of course, either a machine or bench at which a hand craftsman works. Each of these is in the position of a little shop carrying on one little special industry, paying rent for the floor space occupied, interest for the capital involved, depreciation for the wear and tear, and so on, *quite independently of what may be paid by other production centers* in the same shop. ...The cost of each production center is, of course, laden onto the work by a rate per hour. ...Unlike the averaging methods, almost any actual working conditions can be faithfully represented on this system. This is because each production center is virtually independent of any other, and therefore complexity is indifferent to it.[9]

Furthermore, the analogy demonstrated the effect of idle time and allowed Church to introduce the supplementary rate concept.

...Now if the mechanic in one of these shops is only working half time, it is pretty clear that he must double his rate of distribution on such work as he does, if he is to distribute his month's rent over his month's work. But, instead of doubling his rate, he might continue to charge at the normal rate, and then at the month end find how much he was yet in arrear, and distribute this undistributed amount only as a *supplementary rate*. In this way he would benefit in two ways. First, his normal rate being constant, he can compare costs of jobs worked on at different periods; and secondly, the amount of the supplementary rate, (its ratio to the normal rate) will serve as a very accurate barometer of the conditions under which he has been working at any period. ...

...

The meaning of the term supplementary rate will now be understood. It is this which is the invaluable complement to the machine rate and which makes the great distinction between the new method and the old machine-rate method. *The supplementary rate is the undistributed balance of shop charges due to idleness of production centers.*[10]

The supplementary rate took an another important use in Church's definition of it. "The ratio of the supplementary rate to the amount distributed by the machine rates forms a varying barometer, whose fluctuation is an index to the current efficiency of the shop."[11]

Moreover, Church proposed a solution to the problem of direct laborers who work on more than one machine at the same time.

The plan advocated here involves perhaps considerable breaking away from traditions. Briefly speaking, it is proposed in the case of automatic machines to consider wages of attendance as a factor of the new machine rate, based on the *maximum number of machines that can be worked simultaneously under the most favorable conditions.*[12]

He then gave an illustration of his beginning system—as can be seen in Figure 4 on the next page.[13]

Church's next major concept in *The Proper Distribution* would bedevil him for many years. How could one highlight office and selling expenses as well as control them? "...(S)hop charges do not by any means exhaust the whole of the expense account," Church wrote "... there is a large section of expenses incurred in advertising, warehousing, packing, transporting, and conducting the commercial process incident to selling the finished product. These expenses should not on any account be mingled with those due to production."[14] He stressed the dollar significance of these items[15] and felt that some action, however arbitrary, must be taken.

> It is not practicable to isolate the expenditure on advertising, traveling, and so forth so as to debit each piece with the amount incurred on the selling of it; we have therefore to compromise the matter, and compensate the faults of the basis by a classification method which will enable us to discriminate between various classes of products. Even then there is a choice between three bases of value on which the general charge may be distributed.
> General charges may be distributed: 1, on wages cost only; 2, on works cost; 3, on an hourly basis, according to the number of hours consumed in the production.[16]

Church ended the book with a classic statement of his philosophy towards the inevitably growing complexity of modern industry. Simplicity was a constant danger.

> A few final observations may be offered on the subject of works accounting generally. Modern methods have taken their rise in the growing complexity of modern industry. They, like the industry itself, tend to become more complicated in proportion as the numbers of their factors increase. The snare of the "simple system" must therefore be avoided. One cannot calculate the weight of the earth or the distance of Uranus by means of common arithmetic. Nor can anyone represent the thousand-and-one interlocked factors of a modern factory by means of a double-entry ledger and an office boy. And just as the whole science of navigation hinges on higher mathematics, so the management of considerable business turns upon intricate principles which are the horror of the rule-of-thumb man and the sheet anchor of the progressive man of business. Now one can traverse the Atlantic in an open boat and without the Nautical Almanac, but it is done more quickly and more surely in the Mauretania.[17]

In his classic study *Evolution of Cost Accounting to 1925*, published in 1954, S. Paul Garner included 62 references to Church within the index—an amount that far exceeded references to anyone else.[18] Since Garner's book remains "a primary work for instruction and reference in the area of management accounting,"[19] this is no small feat on the part of Church.

Garner considered Church to be the forerunner of american writers on the subject of the burden element of cost.[20] Recently, Garner reaffirmed his admiration for Church's writing to the writer of this monograph. Garner, in his book, highlighted the tie-in Church made between factors of production and production centers.

> The first interesting feature of Church's new technique was concerned with the proper incidence of shop charges. It was his idea that these could be narrowed down in large part to six or seven "factors," such as land, building, and power, to give three examples. That is to say, a large proportion of indirect charges were not so general as commonly believed. In fact, he would subdivide practically all these charges, leaving only a relatively small amount to be divided on a strictly arbitrary basis. This narrowing down was to be carried only so far as was profitable, and each firm would have to decide that for itself. After the "factors" had been determined, the plant was to be divided into what he called "production centers." These were not necessarily departments in the ordinary interpretation of the term; they might be a series of machines or workbenches.[21]

Garner also related examples of major attacks on Church's idea for the charge of idle time to jobs.

Figure 4
Shop Charges Account

SHOP-CHARGES ACCOUNT (NOVEMBER).

Debit.		Credit.	
To Interest on machine.........	$53.00	By Machine earnings.........$292.53	
" Depreciation on machine.......	53.00	As Table A	
" Power..........	62.00	" Supplementary rate........	305.47
" Wages on auto machines...... (1 operator and overlooker)	55.00	$305.47 Hrs. 2,187 = 14 cts. per hour.	
" Process sundries (oil, etc.)......	25.00		
" Debit for floor burden........	250.00		
" Supervision.....	100.00		
	$598.00		$598.00

Total hours made as Table A = 2,187. Supplementary rate this month = 14 cents per hour. Average hourly burden on hourly-burden plan would be $\frac{598}{2,187}$ = 27.3 cents per hour.

TABLE A. — SHOWING MACHINE TIME MADE AND MACHINE EARNINGS IN NOVEMBER.

No. of Machine.	Total Hours Worked in Month.	(New) Machine Rate Per Hour.	Earnings (i.e. Amts. debited to jobs per Machine Rate.	Remarks.
1.........	130	4 cents.	$5.20	
2.........	125	7 cents.	8.75	
3.........	86	23 cents.	19.78	
4.........	140	25 cents.	35.00	
5.........	200	12 cents.	24.00	
6.........	200	10 cents.	20.00	
7.........	200	9 cents.	18.00	
8.........	90	34 cents.	30.60	
9.........	200	4 cents.	8.00	
10.........	80	16 cents.	12.80	
11.........	....	....	......	
12.........	....	....	......	This group was idle and operator stopped.
13.........	....	....	......	
14.........	....	....	......	
15.........	....	....	......	
16.........	....	....	......	
17.........	140	15 cents.	21.00	
18.........	80	15 cents.	12.00	
19.........	96	15 cents.	14.40	
20.........	140	15 cents.	21.00	
21.........	140	15 cents.	21.00	
22.........	140	15 cents.	21.00	
Totals	2187		$292.53	

COST STATEMENT OF SAME JOB (NOVEMBER).

31 hours' machine time (details as before).............	$4.93
Supplementary rate, 31 hours at 14 cents.............	4.34
TOTAL SHOP CHARGES.......	$9.27
19 hours' wages (details as before)...................	4.12
TOTAL No. 2 OR WORKS COST OF JOB.................	$13.39

The method employed by Church for the disposition of his supplementary rate was also sharply criticized by William Kent, an American consulting engineer, at about this same time. Darlington and Greshom Smith had already suggested that the idle time factor was not a part of the cost of the product, as Church had advocated, but Kent elaborated upon their viewpoints considerably. He insisted that the supplementary rate was not really, as Church had written, an index of the efficiency of the factory; but rather it was a measure of the condition of the business in general, and particularly of the efficiency of the selling division of the firm.[22]

Garner also felt that "Church was more interested in the theoretical aspects of the method and neglected to give much attention to the ledger treatment."[23]

Murray Wells is another writer who recognized the value of Church's first major work. Wells both commented on Church and gave bibliographical references to other's comments on him in a three book series, published as Monograph 10 in 1978 by the Center for International Education and Research in Accounting at the University of Illinois.[24] Two of these books—A Bibliography of Cost Accounting: Its Origins and Development to 1914, Parts I and II—were companion volumes to his Accounting for Common Costs, "an historical review of the origins and reasons for the allocation of overhead and other common or joint costs."[25] Wells devoted 12 pages to Church in Accounting for Common Costs.[26]

Like Garner, Wells was impressed with Church's expansive use of the little shop analogy to develop the production center concept, with his criticism of the direct labor cost method of allocating overhead, and with his drawing attention to the effects of idle time.[27] However, Wells felt that "Church was not generally supported in his proposal to allocate office and selling expenses,"[28] and that he was quite vague in respect to the purposes to be achieved by his system for factory costs.[29] For instance, Wells noted that Church did not, however, demonstrate how his system produced information which was a necessary part of that required for control, decision making, or inventory valuation."[30] Wells ended with the following comment about Church's work.

> Church has been singled out for particular attention because he was unique in several respects. He had experience of British systems of accounting, under Slater Lewis, before migrating to the United States about 1900. More than his American predecessors, he emphasized accounting as well as purely costing matters. He attempted to justify all aspects of the system he described, not just to explain its operation. His writings therefore provide the opportunity of illustrating the shortcoming of even the best writing of the period. This should not be construed however, as suggesting that nothing worthwhile emerged from Church's or other engineers' works...[31]

Throughout the two volume bibliography, Wells included notes on those who referenced Church's 1901/1908 works. In 1902, Charles Carpenter stated that Church proposed one of the most thorough and exact systems of distribution yet presented and John Whitmore considered Church's work exceedingly valuable, relatively exhaustive, and very fully considered.[32] Whitmore later mentioned his indebtedness to Church.[33] Gershom Smith in The Engineering Magazine wrote that"...Mr. Church has an 'ideal' system which to one who has carefully studied the situation is simply a machine-rate system scientifically applied..."[34] J. Gilmore Williamson was somewhat positive about the machine rate approach, as it was preferable to having a different rate of on cost for each department. However, "Mr. Church's scientific theory 'that every dollar of charges must be burdened on to some item of work in costing is absurd'. Cost and Establishment charges should be dealt with separately..."[35]

In 1952, David Solomons reviewed the 1901 writings of Church, emphasizing Church's idea of production centers.[36] In his analysis, Solomons did a fine job of summarizing Church's machine rate approach.

> He turns to the machine-hour rate of earlier days only to dismiss it as hopelessly crude. But it does have one advantage over other methods: it does take into account the variation

in the cost of work done on different types of machine. It is this idea which Church takes and develops. "What does the expression 'shop' really signify?" he asks. We get no nearer to disentangling costs so long as we look at the shop as an organic whole. But if we regard it as a collection of "little shops" or production centres, the problem suddenly becomes clear. Each "little shop," consisting of a machine, or a bench at which a handcraftsman works, must be charged with its own depreciation, rent, and other running expenses. The cost of each production centre is then loaded on to the work passing through it, at an hourly rate, which he calls the "scientific machine rate."[37]

Although he was critical of Church's supplementary rate idea, Solomons suggested that Church's idea did stimulate other to do better—notably John Whitmore in 1906.[38]

> It is, or course, easy to criticize Church's "supplementary rate." In the first place, the net effect on job costs was to bring them back to the "actual costs" which they would have shown, had the "scientific" machine rate and the supplementary rate not been kept separate in the first place. Second, the fact that the supplementary rate was made up not only of unabsorbed machine expenses but also of the unallocable general shop expenses made nonsense of Church's claims that the supplementary rate was a barometer of shop efficiency: for a rise in the general expenses would raise the supplementary rate even if all machines were being fully utilized. Even a rise in allocable machine expenses caused by sharp rise in the price-level would raise the supplementary rate irrespective of the degree of capacity usage....[39]

Sir Charles Renold, the son of Hans Renold, wrote a very revealing article, "Management Accounts," in 1950 about Church and the Renold Company shortly after the turn of the century.[40] Sir Charles joined the company in 1905, when there were no monthly statements but an intense interest in costs as there was a necessity to bid on each job.[41] He apparently never met Church, as Sir Charles thought that Church's system was imported from America by Hans Renold.[42] Sir Charles accurately described the system,[43] which was contained in the 1901 articles by Church.

> When I entered the business this system was in its first full flush of enthusiasm. It was developed and refined over the next few years until it became quite unmanageable in its ramifications, elaborations and adjustments. It could never be kept up-to-date and even if it were up-to-date the costs which it turned out, though possibly factually sound, were in a form that gave no convenient guide to action. In producing a cost, bits and pieces of every conceivable kind of expense had gone into the pan and, though each had contributed its flavour, the resulting omelet could not be unscrambled for examination.[44]

The system was re-examined in 1910 and a new system evolved by 1915. The purposes were to tie-in better to the actual expense and to get a more accurate accounting for general overhead, which had greatly increased in significance.[45] The revamped Church system broke down during World War I, in which there was a need to make too many adjustments.[16]

The writer's visit to Renold Ltd. yielded a tangible reward. The illustrations found on the next two pages—Figure 5, Part 1 and Part 2—depict the overall flow of the machine hour rate system. The figure represent, in the writer's opinion, an excellent graphical portrayal of that system.

In his 1957 publication, *Overhead Costing: The Costing of Manufactured Products*,[47] R. Lee Brumnet credited Church with paving the way for the development of concepts on standard overhead costs of products.[48] Brummet wrote:

> Church, in emphasizing a residual to be distributed by use of a supplementary rate, had stressed the significance of the amount as an index of utilization of plant facilities and thus had also introduced the concern for managerial usefulness of cost information. With this basic idea introduced, it was only a slight additional step to consider other costs which might, if divorced from product assignments, provide useful indicators of productive effectiveness.[49]

Figure 5 Part I

Diagram of Cost System

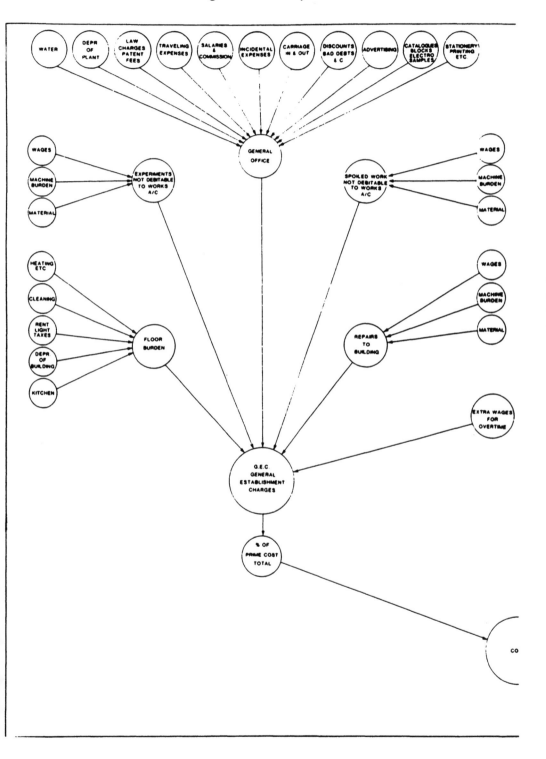

Figure 5 Part II

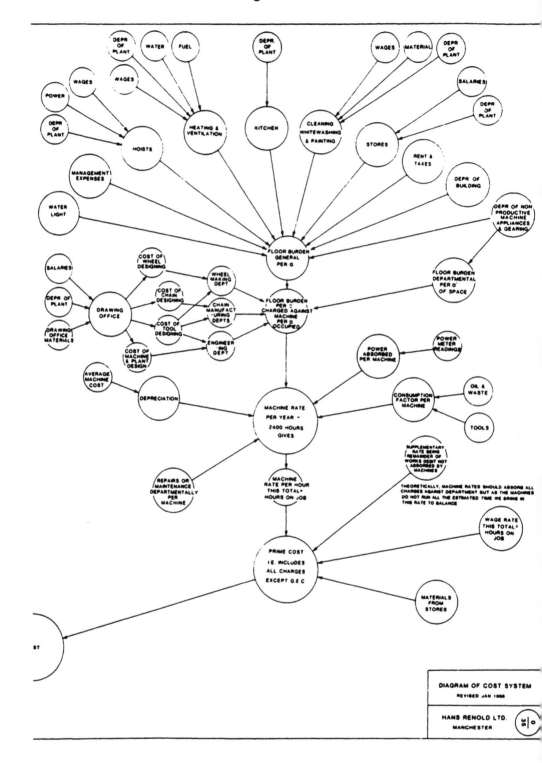

Brummet emphasized that at about the turn of the century, overhead was ignored and product costing was on only direct materials and direct labor.[50] According to Brummet, J.S. Lewis was a major proponent of that view of product costing.[51] Little attention was also given to the problem of idle time costs, until Church's writings of 1901. Brummet claimed that those influential writings inspired the works of David Cowen, H.S. Garry, and John Whitmore.[52]

Litterer, while primarily reviewing Church's management works, did make some interesting comments about Church and his views of overhead.

> ...Church's particular item of interest was overhead accounts. Not too long before Church began writing, overhead had been considered an item of waste, something to eliminate if at all possible, or if this were not feasible, to reduce as much as possible, treating the remainder as a loss. Church took the view that overhead expenditures represented a legitimate type of expense which one should try to see used in the most efficient manner. He turned to the question, what did the expense or overhead account really represent? His analysis of its content and how it should be allocated brought to him the realization that the overhead was intimately associated with the function of management in several ways. On one hand the wages of the firms' executives and managerial personnel were represented directly in the overhead account. Most of the other items in the account reflected important and long-term decisions by management. How well the overhead expenses were used was largely a matter of how efficiently the management was doing its job.[53]

As the writer mentioned in the introduction to this monograph, he is convinced that certain themes started by Church in his 1901/1908 works continued throughout his writings. Clearly, one of these themes is the machine-hour rate method, a concept that Church considered to be his own. even though he gave credit to others for an earlier concept of it.[54] Interestingly, Brummet stressed that Lewis had considered product costs just to contain direct materials and direct labor. Church then would have made a major break from his early mentor on the issue of recognizing overhead as a product cost. As we shall see, Church never let go of what turned out to be a winning concept. He spent years developing and promulgating it. One must admire how Church wove the three thoughts of the production center, the little machine shop analogy, and the factors of production into a very neat system.

As mentioned in the Preface, the writer and a colleague, Henry Schwarzbach, have presented a similar system for accounting as it pertains to robotics. Like Church, they have had many successes with the system. Again, the 1908 Chart from the Renold Company—Figure 5, Part 2, is an excellent representation of the system.

As listed in the first chapter, the writer has highlighted Church's writings into 125 ideas. The first three ideas are related to the machine hour-rate system. [Idea 1] Overhead is a product cost. [Idea 2] The machine-hour rate method is a far superior method of accounting for overhead in a highly capital-intensive firm than other methods of overhead accounting. [Idea 3] The production center is the lowest level of collection of accounting data and might be just one machine.

Most likely, Church envisioned himself as the Charles Babbage of the early 20th Century. When it came to the topic of machinery, Church was a "Renaissance Man." He was vitally concerned with machinery in its multifaceted effects on accounting, management, workers, industrial engineers, production controllers, and society. The exciting world of robotics needs a synthesizer like Church to rationalize the robot into society. [Idea 4] The machine should be the focal point of management efforts.

Church had a consuming interest in control. Techniques had to be refined to replace the old-fashioned "rule-of-thumb" approach of the past. He was willing to give a vague solution to G.E.C. (General Establishment Charges) items just so some attention would be given to them. He may never have developed the control features of his accounting systems to the extent that he did with his management concept of control but his philosophy of accounting as a crucial part of overall managerial control does come through in his efforts. [Idea 5] Accounting is a vital part of managerial control.

Perhaps as a response to the very competitive and bid oriented business world of the late 19th Century and early 20th Century, Church insisted that each job should bear a share of all costs, including G.E.C. items. Ideally, a profit figure could be calculated for each item. [Idea 6] All costs should be recorded, allocated to jobs, and be recovered in the selling price.

Undoubtedly as another consequence of his interest in Babbage, Church took a very broad point of view to the imputation of interest on capital to his accounting system for overhead. While the imputation of interest is a part of his 1901/1908 efforts, Church never fully explained his philosophy on the imputation of interest until later. [Idea 7] Imputed interest on capital is an overhead cost to the firm.

He forever maintained his opposition to the simplistic methods of overhead application based on direct labor dollars and direct labor hours. His direct assaults on the direct labor approaches were excellent but need to be repeated today and tomorrow, time after time. Church was concerned in the very early 20th Century about the facts of increasing overhead costs and decreasing direct labor costs. [Idea 8] Direct labor approaches to overhead allocation are disastrous. [Idea 9] Overhead is growing, while direct labor costs are shrinking.

The supplementary rate approach was designed to highlight idle time of machinery. Utilization of plant capacity was a fetish of his, much more than how to account for it on the financial records. [Idea 10] Machines must not be idle. [Idea 11] Accounting should immediately highlight idle machines and, hence, idle capacity.

Church also showed three weaknesses that would continue through his writing career. One of these was his lack of understanding and, perhaps, concern about the field of financial accounting and about financial accountants. He gave hints of this lack of feeling by such comments as "but the mischief is not only done by that time,"[55] when discussing the broad results of a half-year's work and "figures will prove anything, 'except facts.'" [56] Church seemed to have no interest in the final product reported in financial accounting. Perhaps part of this is Church's use of the rhetorical device of strawmen, as already mentioned in the brief discussion about Taylor. For whatever reasons, Church's lack of sympathy and, perhaps, of knowledge of the uses of financial accounting probably were at the time and more so now a severe detriment to the adoption of his ideas. For example, he never would have gotten so embroiled in the supplementary rate and general establishment quagmires if he had financial accountants and financial accounting in mind.

A second weakness was an overconcern with complexity in his overhead accounting systems. One gets the impression that Church would have been much more successful with his machine hour rate approach if he had come to grips with the complexity of too many different factors of production being accounted in his system. He may not have known enough about accounting to appreciate when a seemingly never-ending list of factors of production do not meet the cost/benefit test for an overall accounting reporting system. However, it is very conceivable that modern counting technology make many of Church's complexities a plus for today and not a minus.

The third weakness is related to the second, and that is the failure to use a simple journal entry to account for the transaction. Church used debits and credits but never in the simple manner of a journal entry. It is almost as if Church had made a policy of never using the traditional format of the journal entry.

However, two positive points offset the negatives. Church was an exceptional writer, and he was an expert in designing charts, graphs, diagrams, and other means of presenting a system. Both abilities served him and his readers well.

1909/1910

The book, *Production Factors in Cost Accounting and Works Management*, is actually a reprint of Church's six articles—published back in 1909. As such, these articles are not reviewed separately.

Church continued to stress the importance of overhead. Very many concerns have come to grief by ignoring the relative importance of the other factors of production.[57] "But in modern work, so it(direct labor) ceases to be the only factor of production, and in the extreme case of a roomful of nearly automatic machinery, may cease even to be an important factor."[58]

In this very stinging comparison of engineers to accountants, the accountants definitely lost.

> The error which dominates and vitiates all the usual and popular methods of dealing with indirect expense is simply "analysis." That is the work on which they all flounder. For the purpose of the accountants this analysis is sufficient, because the accountant is concerned neither with the efficiency nor the improvement of production.
>
> It does not matter greatly to him whether a particular item of expense is due to inefficient power distribution, or to worn-out machinery, or to buildings imperfectly adapted to their uses. To him an expense is an expense, but to the production engineer it may be more than an expense—it may be a revelation. Yet, as long as we persist in looking on all activity and all the expenditure going on in and about a works as due to production, so long will the accountant's point of view necessarily hold the field. As long as we shut our eyes to the fact that actual production is the last organization in a chain of separate organizations so long will the present confused ideas about indirect expense or establishment charges hold their ground unshaken.[59]

Next, Church listed the five uses of cost information.

> But if our costs represent all the actual facts of production and the actual results of our form of organization, then there are several uses which may be made of them. Amongst these may be mentioned:
>
> 1. The financial or accountancy use, as showing how money was expended.
> 2. Comparison with estimated results, as in Mr. Emerson's method, the discrepancy between estimated and actual results being regarded as "preventable waste."
> 3. The technical use, showing the cost of every process on every part, enabling a close check to be made upon efficiency of production.
> 4. Use as a basis for fixing premium or bonus rates.
> 5. The commercial use, as a basis for fixing remunerative prices, and for selecting that class of product that can be most profitably manufactured.[60]

Church wrote that the cost of a process on a single part becomes a perfectly definite and tangible thing and can be recorded as such. The tendency to regard burden or indirect expense as something that should be averaged, manipulated or juggled with, disappears.[61] He utilized "fairness" in his argument for machine rates. "Machine rates differ in proportion as machines are large, heavy, and costly, or small, light, and cheap. If we set the larger of the two in motion, on whatever job, it is just as fair that the job should bear the cost, as it is fair that the job should bear the cost of the higher wage rate of an expensive man."[62]

A notion of many different factors of production, rather than just direct labor and direct materials, was introduced. He remains somewhat unique in this stressing of a many factors of production mode of analyzing costs. "In the method of organization by production factors it is sought *to isolate as many as possible of the special functions exercised by the manufacturer, to determine their steady and regular rent value, by foreseeing their fluctuations, and to charge these rents as regular production factors of perfectly determinable value.*" These factors were diagrammed as shown in Figure 6.[63]

The concept of supplementary rate was further clarified.

> ...No doubt one of the reasons why the practical mind has looked coldly on all burden-distributing systems is an unconscious perception that they cease to mean anything definite as soon as there is any departure from full time and normal working.[64]
>
> It must not be overlooked that the ratio of wasted to utilized capacity is, in itself, a most important and significant figure, and if the production-factor method did nothing more than make this ratio known it would give advantages not otherwise to be attained.[65]
>
> Generally speaking, there falls into the supplementary rate all expenditures for which no return is obtained. Examples of this sort of outlay are suggested in the items listed below. This list is not exhaustive, but will indicate the class of expense so treated. The rate being primarily a waste rate, all expenditure in the nature of dead loss falls into it.

Figure 6

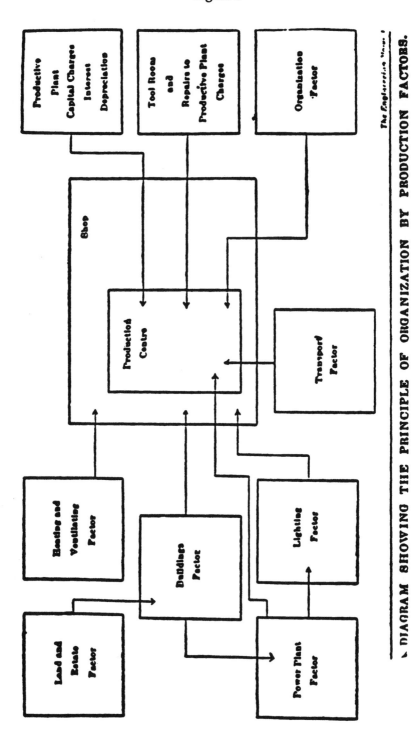

Shop

Production Centre

Productive Plant
Capital Charges
Interest
Depreciation

Tool Room
and
Repairs to
Productive Plant
Charges

Organisation
Factor

Transport
Factor

Heating and
Ventilating
Factor

Buildings
Factor

Lighting
Factor

Land and
Estate
Factor

Power Plant
Factor

A DIAGRAM SHOWING THE PRINCIPLE OF ORGANIZATION BY PRODUCTION FACTORS.

The Engineering News

Idle machine incidence
Spoiled work
Removals and rearrangements of plant, fixtures, etc.
Loss caused by stoppage of power plant
"Extra" payment for overtime[66]

Church presented another diagram to illustrate the factors of production.[67] (See Figure 7). When explaining the diagram. Church noted that "The object of the diagram is, however, merely to give a graphic realization of the way in which different machines absorb factors in different proportions, and it also serves to demonstrate how very far from the truth any 'averaging' system of distributing burden must be."[68] After discussing the diagram (Figure 7). Church went on to present his schedule of Shop Factors and Machine Rates.[69] [See Figure 8.]

He was quite interested in fixed/variable relationships: "The general object of these control accounts is to determine the fixed elements of annual cost of each service, forecast the variable elements, and keep a close watch on the correspondence between the forecast and the actual expenditure. Further they provide a means of equalizing intermittent kinds of expenditure and making it bear fairly and equally on the work."[70] He was indifferent to whether the ending balance of the "Shop Waste or Balancing Account" was closed by either "as a percentage figure of the amount distributed...or the balance may be distributed on an hour basis."[71] The supplementary rate was not to be assigned to specific jobs but to all jobs for the month on the basis of total costs for each job.[72]

As Church explains, the factor type of classification and cost behavior made projections very feasible. "The extent of gain to be made by intensifying production can be ascertained or forecast without any special searching or analysis. The components of every production factor, and also of every machine rate, being always preserved separate and distinct, the relative influence of such charges can be read almost as in an open book."[73] In addition to being interested in cost projections and control, Church was "in favor of isolating overtime operations from those of normal working, a process which would certainly make a very interesting study possible."[74]

Church had some specific comments on the relationship between cost and financial accounting.

> To rely upon an arbitrary established percentage which may actually be either much over, or much under, the real incidence of a number of varied factors on a particular order, may be a good way of getting rid of figures and giving an air of finality to cost accounts, but it is very little else. As a guide to actual profitableness of particular classes of work it is valueless and even dangerous.[75]
> ...To allow the incidence of such wasted resources to become attached to work by means of an averaged percentage, on whatever basis the latter is calculated, is grotesque in its inadequacy to represent actual facts.[76]
> ...No facts that are in themselves complex can be represented in fewer elements than they naturally possess. While it is not denied that many exceedingly complex methods are in use that yield no good results, it must still be recognized that there is a minimum of possible simplicity that cannot be reduced without destroying the value of the whole fabric. The snare of the "simple system" is responsible for more inefficiency and loss than is generally recognized.[77]

He was very explicit that selling expense was to be excluded from manufacturing costs. "The two have no relation whatever to one another," Church emphasized.[78] Nevertheless, he showed great interest in controlling selling expenses; these costs were also to be analyzed.

> It is the more important that this fact be fully realized, since the types of selling organization are far more varied than those of manufacturing organization. Even in the same concern some of the product may be on an entirely different footing as regards selling expense from other items. For example, a large section of the business may consist of a standard product for which there is a steady demand, arising from the reputation of the firm for that product, and requiring no special and expensive efforts to secure business. Another portion may consist of a specialty, recent introduced, and taking a large amount of time,

Figure 7

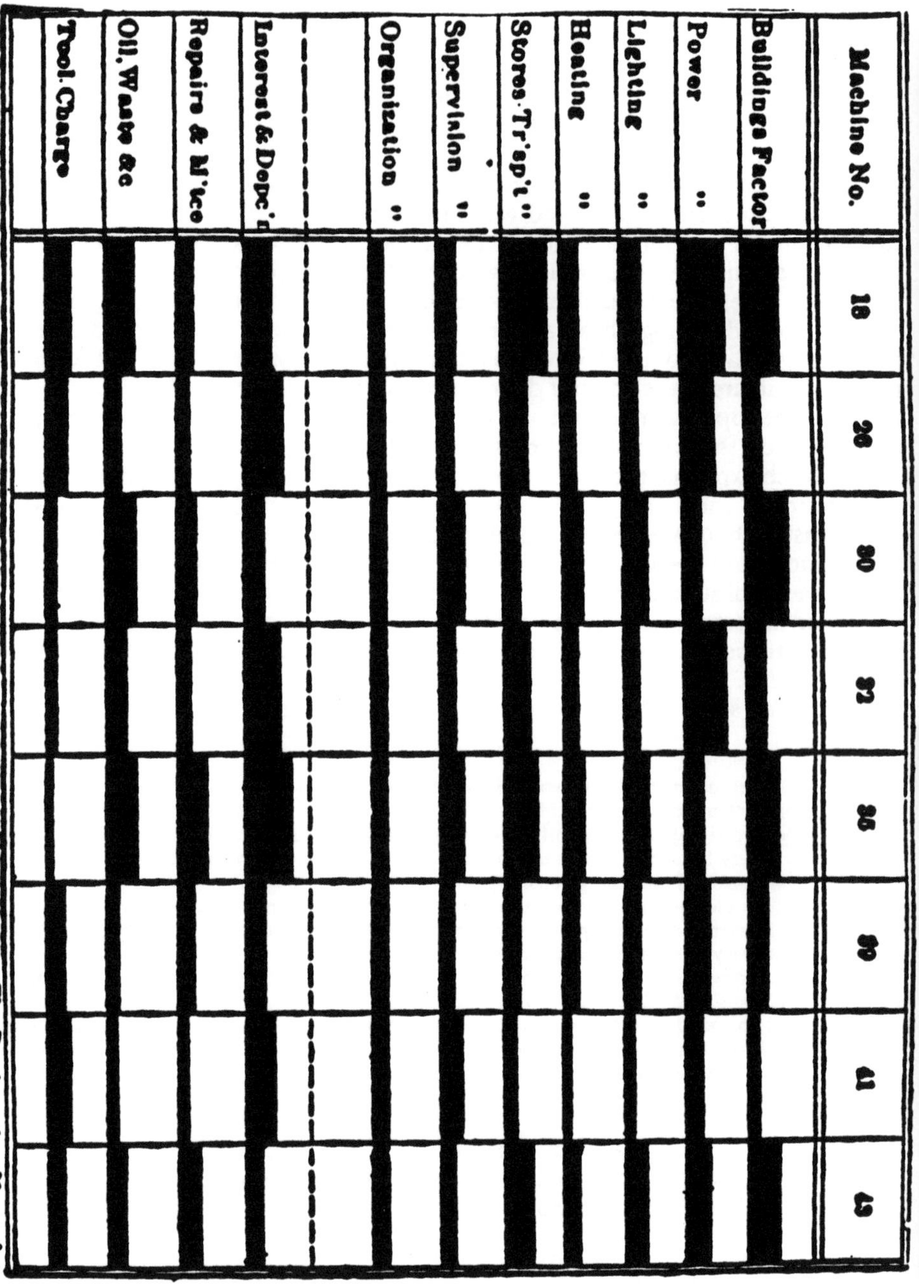

DIAGRAM SHOWING RELATIVE ABSORPTION OF FACTORS
BY THE DIFFERENT PRODUCTION CENTRES IN A SHOP.

Figure 8

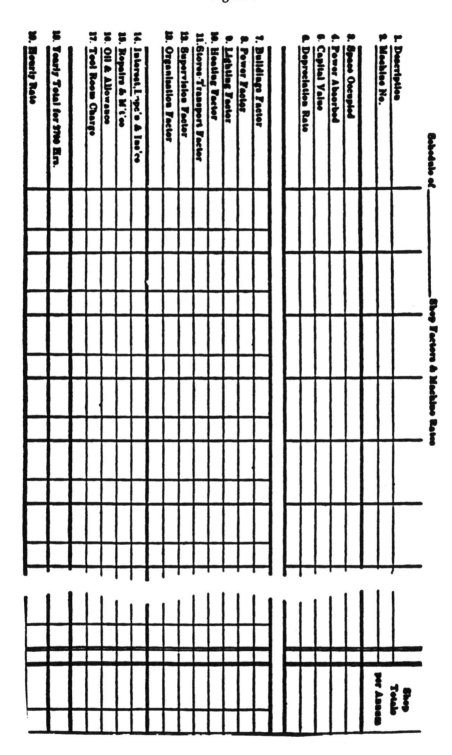

attention, advertising and demonstrating expense, installations on approval, etc., to effect sales.[79]

Furthermore, Church offered a premonition of things to come in standard costs.

> ...Only the accumulation of records and of compared experience can make this possible, but it will be allowed that *a general acceptance of the principle of organization by production factors would have the effect of making known the usual or standard values of such factors under conditions of good practice*, and that therefore as soon as the elements of cost, power, durability, space, and attendance of any new machine were determined, *its nominal rate under conditions of efficiency and economical installation and working would also be predeterminable with sufficiently close accuracy.*[80]

Garner was kind on some of Church's points, but not so kind on other ideas. Church's writings on the production factor method were considered to be "so ably expounded,"[81] for example, whereas Church's handling of the supplementary rate issue was in Garner's view, not particularly convincing.

> ...It should be noted that he still called the idle time charge an "expense," and that he at this point made it clear that the desirable practice was to apportion the "idle time expense" to processed goods, and not to close it out to profit and loss as an outright loss.
> Yet in another place in the same book he recommended that the individual job orders not be charged with any portion of the supplementary rate... Church advocated that it be shown only on each "work order as a whole on its monthly total and not upon its constituent jobs." This seemed to conflict with the procedure described above,...[82]

Yet, Garner felt that Church modified his position on selling and administrative expenses as job costs, and that, by 1910, clearly favored a charge to profit and loss for these expenses.[83]

Wells spent a good deal of time attacking Church's system in a detailed analysis that compares the system to the five uses of cost information listed by Church himself.[84]

> As long as the accounts described by Church were to be used by an owner/manager, little harm could result from the arbitrariness and subjectivity described above. When, however, those accounts were used by one manager to inform another, or by managers to inform investors, then the accounts lost the attribute of reliability usually accorded factual statements. If the accounts could be varied at will either through altering an allocation base of method, or through changing cost imputations, then they could not be claimed to be serving any of the purposes listed by Church. Those purposes would only be served, as Church himself pointed out, if the "costs represent the actual facts of production and the actual results of our organization."[85]

But Wells did also take the time to quote the praises of contemporary admirers of Church. For example, Wells reported that Going, the editor of *The Engineering Magazine*, considered Church to be one of the leading authorities on the distibution of expense burden.[86] And Frazier agreed with Church that the production cost method of pro-rating sales expense is fundamentally unsound.[87] Thanks to Church, Green developed factor costs for buildings as proposed by Hamilton Church.[88] As Bentley astutely commented:

> One may criticize some of Mr. Church's ideas, but the test of the critic is his capacity for devising better ideas. In the opinion of the present writer Mr. Church gives us the ideas toward which we should be working, although modifications may be deemed advisable at times.[89]

Wells notes that Bunnell was critical of Church's supplementary method: "Though this method gets rid of the deficit, it is impossible to defend a system of considering last month's losses as an item of next month's costs. Further, since loss by idle time of one machine is thus covered by increasing the burden-rate of the others, the loss by keeping a big machine for occasional jobs only is effectually concealed."[90] But in equally convincing terms, Smith and Pickworth endorsed the machine rate: "It is difficult to conceive of any method which will give better results from a theoretical point of view."[91]

Galloway affirmed the value of the machine rate as well. In his review of the 1910 book, he wrote that the machine hour rate method "comes nearer to presenting a complete understanding as well as a means of control of the process of manufacture, than any heretofore given."[92] However, Galloway must have sensed the controversy about the level of detail demanded by Church. "No matter how much the cost accountant may disagree with the author (Church) as to the practicability of determining actual costs in such minute detail, he must acknowledge the author's criticism of the 'averaging' method as unscientific and as affording a cheap way out of a practical difficulty to be just."[93]

The writer of this monograph believes that Church did an excellent job in the development of his production factors. The machine hour rate method was clearly better tied to the multi-factors of production in the 1909/1910 works than in the 1901/1908 efforts. In fact, Church might have made as important a contribution with his multi-factor approach as his machine hour rate method. If Church had followed up on the multi-factor approach with a clear exposition of machine costs as a fourth accounting classification of production costs system, he might have been successful in causing permanent damage to the direct labor, direct material and overhead troika of traditional cost accounting. [Idea 12] There are many factors of production and [Idea 13] Overhead must be analyzed by factors of production. The next three ideas focused on control of overhead costs. [Idea 14] There should be a comparison of actual cost to standard costs. [Idea 15] Overtime must be controlled. [Idea 16] Fixed/variable analysis is extremely helpful in controlling overhead.

Church clearly did not feel any better about accountants, at least the financial type of accountants, than he did in 1901. He may have over-used the strawman rhetorical device when he said that "the accountant is concerned neither with the efficiency nor the improvement of production."[94] His seeming insensitivity caused him to overlook many opportunities for dialogue on such issues as machine costs as a fourth classification of product costs, accounting for cost of idle time, and accounting for imputed interest. Church should have anticipated such criticisms that would come and best exemplified in Wells' review.

In summary, then, Church's 1910 writings are characterized by several tendencies. He continued with his comparative analysis of complexity versus simplicity. And, he continued his stress upon the importance of machines, including a masterful tie-in of the factors of production with the machine hour rate method. Church's five uses of cost information provided a good list for control purposes. Finally, his attacks on allocation of overhead by the direct labor approaches appeared to be gaining a great deal of support. Notably, too, most would probably agree that Church's charts and diagrams reached their peak in his 1909/1910 effort.

1911, 1912 (article) and 1913

This section covers a potpourri of shorter items written by Church for various purposes. It is important to note that his 1912 writing was neither listed by Urwick nor by *The Accountants' Index*.

Church's paper at the National Machine Tool Builders Association on May 18, 1911 obviously captured the attention of two editors, one from the *American Machinist*[95] and the other from *The Iron Age*.[96] The *American Machinist* article presented the paper in its entirety (with the last two sentences missing) and since that article represented the first opportunity to study a speech by Church, it was the basis for the review, rather than *The Iron Age* article.

He was at the meeting to sell "a new way of looking at the facts of production"[97] and to offer "not so much a specific system of record, as a set of principles, the practical application of which can be and indeed must be varied and adapted to suit individual cases."[98] The system was his revision of the old, arbitrarily fixed, machine rates by his machine rents (machine hour rate method).[99] The theme that increased competition was forcing manufacturers to be concerned about costs was repeated and also repeated was his attack on jumbling costs into a common fund termed expense burden.[100] Church then gave a good synopsis of his philosophy of the management of non-manufacturing functions. "In order to manufacture economically, most manufacturers...take on a number of nonmanufacturing functions, some of which are preliminary to production, such as that of landowner, landlord, or power supplier, and some of which are incurred with, both subsidiary to, production, as, for example, storekeeping and costkeeping."[101] He also stated that "expense burden represents, not the cost of production, but the cost of capacity to produce." "...There is no such thing as expense burden—that there are only a number of separate expenses incurred to maintain various departments of the capacity to produce."[102]

After his typical discussion of idle time, Church then gave a summary of his major elements in the system.

> First, instead of throwing all indirect expenses together into a common fund of burden, and then elaborately analyzing them in the despairing effort to make something significant of them, we segregate and keep separate the cost of all nonmanufacturing services.
> Secondly, having segregated each group of expenses we determine the rent charge that must be made for it, precisely as the owner of a terrace of houses settles what rent he will charge individual tenants. But, of course, in the case of these service rents, there is no item of net profit included.
> Thirdly, each department is charged up with its due share of each of these service rents.
> Fourthly, the share of individual machines in each of these different service rents is ascertained.
> Finally, at the end of this process, each machine will have been found to be charged with a number of annual rent charges, which represent the annual cost of that machine's capacity to produce. These separate charges are aggregated and commuted into an hourly machine rent, which is charged against all work done at that machine.[103]

He claimed his system attains true costs and that the question of idle time costs is "to be determined by bookkeeping considerations which have nothing to do with cost proper."[104]

In a letter to the editor of the *American Machinist*, Church defended his machine rate system against an intruder, the "direct costing" approach in which fixed manufacturing overhead is charged not to the product but as a period cost.[105] Church admitted that the "direct costing" approach, as espoused by Edtterson, was better than "the old-fashioned methods of lumping all the indirect costs into one general fund called burden and then expressing this as a percentage of labor."[106] Still, Church believed that his machine rate approach was favored by most modern authorities on cost accounting.[107] He quoted two experts, Smith and Collins,[108] as examples of such support, and then ended the letter by recommending that Edtterson read his 1908 and 1910 books.[109]

Church's 1913 article on interest as a manufacturing cost was a part of a four article debate on the topic. Cole and Church were arguing for inclusion, while Richards and Sterrett disagreed.[110] The editor of *The Journal Accountancy* considered the four writers as well-known and able advocates.[111] Cole felt that "Businessmen are likely to be misled in the future, as they have in the past, by statements of profit which assume that no cost is involved in the use of capital."[112]

Church differentiated between interest paid for borrowed capital—which would not be charged to the cost of manufacturing—and interest assessed for the use of capital values such as "land, buildings, plant machinery, stores, and work in progress, etc."[113] He advocated an imputation of interest by increasing manufacturing costs and increasing an interest earned account.[114] He felt that his production factors approach had laid the groundwork for the inclusion of imputed interest as a manufacturing cost. He wrote:

> ...Wherever capital is made use of, whether in the power plant, in the erection of buildings, or in the purchase of costly special machinery, the use of such capital has to be paid for, somehow and somewhere. *It is only rational that it should be paid for by just those processes (and therefore those jobs) which involve its use. To exclude interest charge from cost of these jobs is to ignore one of the most important matters that we should know, namely—how far this use of capital is economically justified.*[115]

Church ended with a plea for an involvement of the concept of imputed interest in the procurement of new machinery. "In particular, no purchase of new equipment should be made until its call on all production factors has been worked out, and due attention paid to the influence of its use of capital, as represented by a reasonable interest charge."[116]

Not everyone agreed. Richards felt that imputed interest was usually done either to increase prices or to conceal costs. He thought that depreciation included the interest factor and that financing should be kept separate from operations.[117] Sterrett worried about different rates being used by different companies, about the materiality of the interest charges on certain jobs, and about premature realization of profit.[118]

It has already been noted that Church was a consultant on production control matters at the Winchester Repeating Arms Company in 1916 through 1918.[119] While it is not possible to measure Church's impact on the decision by Winchester to include interest on cost of capital for its ordnance contract with the United States Government,[120] it is interesting to note that imputed interest was allowed in 1917.[121] Apparently, the Federal Government reversed its stand and finally won its case for exclusion in 1931.[122] What is clear, though, is that the topic of imputed interest was not merely an academic one.

Two reviewers commented on Church's articles. While primarily focusing on Church's management writings, Jelinek did review the May 25, 1911 article in her work, "Toward Systematic Management: Alexander Hamilton Church."[123]

> Church's observations on overhead expenses and ancillary tasks form the second major facet of his contribution to the development of administrative systems for systematically managing organizations. Given the notion of specialized managerial labor, planning and coordinating functions, and so on, some means of accounting for these indirect expenses and measuring their impact was essential. Church provided this in his treatment of overhead. The ultimate goal throughout is systematic, coordinated management of the enterprise as a whole.[124]

Brummet did make note of the torrent of debate on the topic of imputed interest. He noted both Church and Scovell as chief proponents of this imputation.

> ...The basis for such argument was primarily in terms of the importance of segregation of interest from profits in the sense utilized by most economists of that day and even of today. This enthusiasm has waned since 1930 and one finds only little favor for Scovell's position at this time (1957). Yet Garner suggests that it seems only to be smoldering, awaiting perhaps a recrudescence.[125]

The writer of this monograph believes that Church began to stress principles rather than specific implementations of overhead accounting. As to be seen in Chapter 5, he was becoming very interested in "principles of management" and in applications of these principles in varying situations. Church also redefined overhead as the cost of capacity to produce. [Idea 17] There are principles of overhead treatment. [Idea 18] The techniques of applying the principles of overhead are going to vary with the situation at hand. [Idea 19] Overhead is the cost of capacity to produce.

He took a very broad view in 1913 of what should be included in the cost of capital. Capital was to include investments in land, buildings, plant machinery, stores, and work in progress. [Idea 20] The cost of capital should be broadly based.

Ironically, as can be seen from his 1912 letter, Church would have been a vociferous opponent of the direct costing school for overhead accounting which blossomed after his death. His 1912 letter to the editor should be included in the accounting literature by an addendum to *The Accountants' Index of 1920*. This writer senses that there was a wealth of accounting literature up to 1920 not included in the index.

Church did finally much better explain his stand on imputed interest and showed his willingness to enter the fray of the public arena on this topic and on the machine-hour rate system with the multi-factor approach added to it. As already mentioned, this willingness to do a public speech casts some doubt on the reticence issue. More importantly, the willingness to spread his views by other means than by articles and books from *The Engineering Magazine* opened up many new avenues for his writings and his influence.

CHAPTER FOUR
ACCOUNTING WRITINGS (PART TWO)

The second part of Church's accounting writings is grouped as follows: 1. 1915; 2. 1917/1929; 3. 1930/1931; and 4. 1934. The 1915 articles are, more accurately, two letters to the editor of the *American Machinist*. The 1917 book and its 1929 revision constitute Church's most complete efforts in accounting. The 1930 book and the 1931 article from it center on overhead issues. The 1934 items are two small sections from the *Cost and Production Handbook*— sections this writer believes Church wrote. These items are, hence, attributions to Church by this writer and are not noted in other sources on Church.

1915

A most interesting exchange took place in the *American Machinist* between Gantt and Church in 1915. The exchange sprang from a June 17, 1915 article, "The Relation Between Production and Costs," by Gantt. Equally interesting is the frequent oversight of this debate. For instance, *The Accounting Index: 1920*, a compilation of all accounting pieces at hand in the library of the old American Institute of Accountants (now the American Institute of Certified Public Accountants),[1] does not list any of these articles in the *American Machinist*.[2]

Gantt's June 17, 1915 article made no reference to Church's efforts. Gantt first declared that "there does not yet seem to have been devised any system of distributing that portion of the expense known variously as indirect expense, burden or overhead, in such a manner as to make us have any real confidence that it has been done properly."[3] He claimed that the direct labor approach, the machine hour approach, or other methods mostly apportioned overhead on actual production, which caused much higher costs per unit in slack times than in good times.[4] Accountants are to blame for this, as they are subservient to financiers, Gantt emphasized.[5] Gantt then stated his general principle that *"The indirect expense chargeable to the output of a factory bears the same ratio to the indirect expense necessary to run the factory at normal capacity, as the output in question bears to the normal output of the factory."*[6] The undistributed balance, as a result, should be closed to profit and loss. This approach "warns us to do everything possible to increase the efficiency of the plant we have, rather than to increase its size."[7] Engineers, not cost accountants, are the ones to determine the general overhead that should be charged.[8]

By this point in the monograph, you would undoubtedly expect that Church responded to Gantt's article. Indeed he did on July 29, 1915. Church commended Gantt for becoming a reformer on the burden issue. "I wish him success, more particularly because for 15 years I have made a special study of that field and have written two books on it that remain, I believe, the only works dealing exhaustively with the principles of burden distribution."[9]

Still, Church cautioned Gantt, pointing out that even though he was correct in following his method of segregating idle time costs, Gantt was on dangerous ground by using an ordinary percentage method to distribute burden.[10] "The only way in which this problem has been solved hitherto is by the 'production factor' method, which gives use to accurately determined individual machine rates and collects all undistributed burden into a 'supplementary rate,'"[11] Church wrote in response to Gantt. Church continued to think that a general charge to production for undistributed burden was to be preferred to a charge to profit and loss.[12] He felt that the charge to profit and loss would encourage the hiding of costs there.[13]

Gantt responded harshly in the August 26, 1915 issue.[14] He served a direct blow to Church by claiming Taylor had beaten Church to the punch.

> He admits that it can be done if the "machine-expense" factor method is used, but seems to feel that because he has been advocating the use of "machine-expense" factors for 15 years and has written two books on the subject that he has a sort of monopoly of it. As a matter of fact, the late Frederick W. Taylor found, nearly 25 years ago, that his attempts at improving methods of manufacture were so hampered by the cost accountant that he was forced himself to become an expert accountant in order to foil their efforts. This he did in his usual thorough manner, and passed on to his followers what he had learned. It was from his teachings in 1897 that I got the idea of "machine-expense" factors, which I have since used whenever I had occasion to do so...[15]

Gantt strongly defended his policy of charging profit and loss for undistributed burden and then proceeded to attack Church still more.[16]

> The fourth item I got out of his article was a feeling of resentment at my statement that an engineer and not an accountant was needed to say what the output of a plant should be. This seems the real cause of his writing the article, for I cannot imagine he really believes me to be as ignorant of the best present methods of cost keeping as he assumes I am. I did not intend to make any criticisms of those cost accountants who confine themselves to their proper work of recording and reporting what has been done but only of those who assume that what has been done in the past is a measure of what can be done in the future. It is at this point that the cost accountant stops and the engineer takes up the work. The cost accountant necessarily looks backward: it is the duty of the engineer to look forward.[17]

Church took another swing at Gantt in this war of words in the September 2, 1915 issue of the same publication. He made light of Gantt's claim that Taylor discovered the machine rate method, pointing out that Taylor's approach was "as yet unpublished, and unknown to the world at large."[18] He defended his supplementary rate charge, as many businesses expect to have some idle capacity and, therefore, must consider this a cost. Church then wrote a very personally revealing paragraph.

> As for Mr. Gantt's imputation that my criticism was due to a feeling of resentment in the old quarrel—engineer versus accountant—this is rather amusing, seeing that I am generally accused of taking precisely the opposite side. From this I am emboldened to fancy that my standpoint is probably pretty nearly an impartial one. I was an engineer before I was an accountant, and as an engineer I obtained a knowledge of what the problem was: but it must be remembered that scientific accounting is a kind of engineering too, being in fact the science of the measurement of values. In cost accounting both these sciences meet, and the principles of both, arising out of special kinds of experience in each case, must be taken into consideration to effect a cure.[19]

Mercifully, the exchange ended with Gantt's reply on the October 21, 1915 issue.[20] Interestingly, he thought Church was setting up a man of straw and then just as industriously trying to knock him down.[21] However, Gantt tried to bring peace by saying that they were not far apart in philosophy of undistributed burden. Perhaps because Gantt was uncertain who had, in essence, "won" the dialogue, he pronounced accord and discrepancy in the same breath. The last paragraph of Gantt's article, therefore, is somewhat of a puzzle.

> I do not think Mr. Church and I are very far apart; but inasmuch as the accountant is, as a rule, "the servant of the financier," he has found it necessary to soften down the results that this method exposes in order to have them accepted by the financier. Mr. Church is really defending his method of putting the unabsorbed expense in a reserve fund to be distributed later, which he practically admits was a concession to the financier. I absolutely fail to see why this reserve fund which is really an "idleness charge," should be spread over the product with which it had nothing to do.[22]

In the September 23, 1915, issue, William McHenry tried to make peace between Gantt and Church, whom he called "my master."[23] McHenry thought Church was correct to insist that if the basis for distributing overhead were incorrect, so would be the amount of undistributed burden. But McHenry shifted his opinion on Church's view of the supplementary rate. When he was first in manufacturing, McHenry agreed with Church's view on the issue, but later he thought differently, and considered the supplementary rate to be "wrong in principle and absurd in practice to add to the true cost of doing a thing the wholly misleading cost of not doing that thing or any other thing."[24] He ended with this paragraph.

> This subject is rapidly assuming the dignity of a science, and past pretensions are melting away. The manufacturer is demanding more ability to forecast and less and less of the historian in his cost man, and I cannot entirely agree with Mr. Gantt that the engineer should have monopoly of the forecasting; rather, I feel that the cost man must recognize his position and see that he has some technical foundation to build upon.[25]

The writer of this monograph considers this exchange as one more example of the snare that Church had gotten himself into with his supplementary rate. But his lack of concern about financial accounting was mild compared to Gantt's complete hatred and ignorance of that subject. What's more important to witness is Church's personal responses. Church's initial comment, that he was first an engineer and is now an accountant, strikes this writer as quite important, particularly since Church never before (or again) labeled himself an "accountant." And, Church's fiercely proud defense, rebuking Gantt's claim that he was not the founder of the machine hour rate method, indicates a spirited nature which runs contrary to Urwick's description of a shy, soft-spoken individual. In the same manner, Church's continued dislike for averaging overhead, as Gantt had done, evinces a character who was not afraid to proclaim that he was right. This exchange also indicates that Gantt, like this writer, considered Church to be well-schooled in the rhetorical device of the strawman. Furthermore, the exchange clearly shows the hostility between the Taylor School and Church. Church was not a disciple of Taylor. Church represented a contrary school of thought.

It probably bears repeating that *The Accountants' Index* of 1920 is obviously incomplete and that a major study should be done now to update it. This study would have the advantage of modern data and word processing machinery and would yield, in the writer's opinion, a tremendous cache of articles not catalogued in that index.

1917/1929

A. Hamilton Church's third accounting book, *Manufacturing Costs and Accounts*, was published in 1917 and was presented in more of a textbook fashion than his first two accounting books, although it clearly was not a traditional textbook with questions and problems at the end of each chapter.[26] Much of this work was a smoothing out of his prior writings in accounting. In 1929, he published a revised and enlarged second edition.[27]

In the preface to the 1917 book, Church provided the reader with a clearly stated theme.

> ...The cost man is rarely an accountant in the full sense of that word. He lives in a world of detail, and is apt to undervalue the broader groupings that alone interest, as a rule, the general accountant. It has been attempted in the present work to show the cost accountant the relation of his work to the general accounts. Further, the peculiar value of detail to the

technical arm has been emphasized with a view to exhibit to the general accountant a viewpoint that he sometimes misses.[28]

Two chapters on the mechanism of accounting and of cost accounting were presented.[29]
He labeled the scientific machine rate plan as Method C and gave an illustration of the sys-
tem, using a relatively unique means. (See Figure 9.)[30]
Church strove to differentiate waste, spoilage, and scrap.

> It will be seen that waste, spoilage and scrap are three separate things:
> Waste is a loss of quantity of product, due to failure to extract the most out of material,
> or to inevitable conditions of manufacture.
> Spoilage is the destruction of material already in process, and carries with it not only
> the value of the material spoiled, but also all the labor and expense that has been expended
> on it up to the time it was condemned.
> Scrap is material of no use for the purpose that the original material was used for. It may
> arise from spoilage, as in the case cited above, but more usually it is a kind of by product
> such as cotton-waste in cotton-spinning, sprues and gates in castings, turnings and filings
> in metal working, the remnants of sheets from which all the possible blanks have been cut
> or stamped, and so forth. It should be noted that scrap from one industry is frequently
> the raw material of another industry. When this happens, higher prices can be obtained
> for such scrap than would be possible otherwise.[31]

He introduced, in this text, a very tight control system for work done in the factory.

> But in the case of such a machine, we should still want some simple and effective method
> of viewing the cost of the detailed processes and of the material used as a single group.
> In other words though we want great detail, we also want the detail of this order kept en-
> tirely separate from the detail of other orders. Some method must, therefore, be devised
> of identifying the order as a whole and also of identifying the details as well.
> This is effected by issuing a Production Order for the whole machine, and Job, Piece, or
> Component Orders for the individual parts and processes.[32]

The goal of Method C was to identify all expenses with the cost of working *individual
machines*, or "production centers, so that each machine becomes as it were a separate department, with an accurately determined departmental cost."[33] This presented no change from
his previous position. However, he did seem to bend a bit, just a bit, on the question of disposition of unabsorbed burden.

> No clear and general rule can, therefore, be laid down as to whether the cost of wasted
> manufacturing capacity should be distributed over Orders by means of a supplementary
> rate or charged to a Waste account and so to Profit and Loss.[34]

Church had a much more tightly defined time period constraint in his third accounting
book. "Further, these expenses must be *annual* figures. They must represent the whole of
the charges for one year, since items like heating and lighting at any rate will vary in amount
between one part of the year and another. A selected month will, therefore, not meet the
case."[35] He also seemed to be equivocating on the mandating of imputation of interest.

> Interest, therefore, to sum up, is a charge made to non-productive and productive depart-
> ments, through Standing Orders, for the use of capital, and is, of course, in proportion
> to the amount of capital locked up in various forms as enumerated in the Depreciation or
> Interest Schedules. It is a matter of options whether it is included in costs; but if it is not,
> some of the advantages of the more advanced methods of costing are lost. Whether there
> are disadvantages that counterbalance its inclusion on this ground remains at present a
> matter of opinion.[36]

The revised 1929 book included questions at the end of some of the chapters and did include a new topic, departmentalization.[37] Church classified departments as either service
or productive departments.[38] He did include a tighter presentation of factors of production—

Figure 9
Costing on Method C

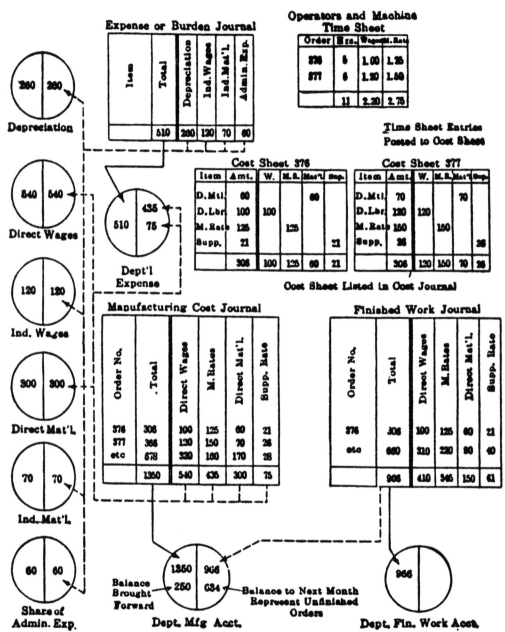

—Costing on Method C.   Direct labor charged to order numbers.
Expense charged to order numbers through machine rates.   Undistributed
expense (due to idle machines or wasted manufacturing capacity) prorated
over orders as supplementary rate.

individual (machine) factor, organization factor, supervision factor, stores transport factor, power factor, and space factor.[39] Other than these relatively minor changes, the 1929 book added little new to the 1917 book, in this writer's opinion.

Critics such as Garner, however, remarked on the differences which pleased them and bothered them. Garner was less than enthralled by Church's handling of the bookkeeping aspects of burden, for instance.

> Also in 1917, A. Hamilton Church, who had first given his views in 1901, summarized more completely his preferred method, of handling the burden items. The charges were first to be debited to individual accounts, just as he had previously recommended; but periodically, through the means of a burden journal, they were to be transferred to departmental burden accounts, as debits in total. From the departmental burden accounts, which were not control accounts, the amounts applied to goods in process were to be transferred, this time through a manufacturing journal, to departmental manufacturing accounts, one for each department. Church thus used a rather roundabout device for securing the desired control over burden without actually using true control accounts at all. This might have proved more cumbersome in practice than some of the methods or techniques already recommended.[40]

However, Garner was much more positive on Church's discussion of waste, spoilage, and scrap,[41] primarily because it lead into a further discussion of accounting for by-products.[42]

> ...By 1917, for example, A. Hamilton Church felt it necessary to make a most careful distinction as to the difference between waste, spoilage, scrap, and by-products, as a prerequisite to their correct handling on the books of the factory. While adding very little that was new to the subject, Church's discussion was perhaps the clearest exposition of the problems involved that had appeared up to that time.[43]

On other matters, Garner felt that Church further wavered in 1917 on his stand on the disposition of unabsorbed burden by the supplementary rate technique. While Church still argued for the allocation to production orders, he admitted that closing burden to profit and loss was much simpler and, perhaps, in certain cases, to be recommended.[44] It is interesting to note that Garner discussed Church's 1917 views on interest along with those of C. H. Scovell, who wrote *Cost Accounting and Burden Application*[45] and who had employed Church in 1911.[46] Scovell, who shared Church's view on the imputation of interest on capital investment, felt that political economists held the best views on inclusion of interest costs.[47]

In his review of the 1917 book for the *American Machinist*, Kimball spent virtually no time quibbling about Church's "wavering" views. Rather, Kimball expresses geniune praise, lamenting only that Church didn't write more about cost prediction.[48] "It was to be expected that any book by this author, who has contributed so much to the discussion of cost finding, would be worthwhile, and this expectation is fully realized."[49] "...Chapters 19, 20 and 21 are devoted to a discussion of Mr. Church's well known plan of allocating expense by means of a scientific machine rate, so called, and a supplementary rate."[50] The book "...is perhaps...the best statement of the relation of cost finding to the general accounts that has yet appeared."[51] "Even the subject of production centers, which the author is particularly interested, since it is largely his own conception, has been treated concisely."[52] Kimball noted that Church's discussion of the primary principles and mechanisms of cost finding were not as complete as in other cost books but still complete enough to be clear.[53]

A.T. Cameron reviewed the 1917 text and concluded that the book was a notable addition to a cost accounting library and of considerable value to a student well grounded in the basic principles of accounting.[54] Still, he was critical of Church's chapters in the first part of the book.

> Some question may be raised as to the wisdom of attempting to teach or explain the theory of double entry bookkeeping in the small amount of space allotted to this subject by the author in part one. In these days when the accounting profession is trying to establish a satisfactory terminology it is decidedly confusing to the average student to encounter the distinctions that the author makes between journals and books of original entry. One

Harold Dudley Greeley concluded that the 1917 book was a scholarly and complete treatise.[56] But such a conclusion was not arrived at until Greeley finished picking away at Church for carelessness in bookkeeping and financial accounting. The heart of Greeley's criticisms is best displayed in these statements. "...In fact, the chief criticism of the book is that it distinguishes too much between cost accounting and other accounting, and makes little attempt to show modern methods in general accounting. Sometimes the author dismisses such subjects by saying ...'such matters are purely commercial, and for information respecting them, some authority on commercial accounting should be consulted.'"[57] "It is open to question whether the author is wise in attempting to teach or explain the theory of double-entry bookkeeping in a few words..."[58] "...The author's distinction between accounting and bookkeeping is not very enlightening, but his distinction between journals and books of original entry is puzzling and certainly must be misleading to a student who is trained to regard the journal as a book of original entry..."[59]

Charles Buxton Going reviewed the 1917 book in the *Journal of the American Society of Mechanical Engineers*.[60] He stressed that Church had the intent of enabling the cost accountant and the general accountant to understand each other better and to have a greater appreciation of each other's work.[61] The cost accountant should assume control from the general accountant at the factory gate, keep control until the product is finished, and tie-in cost records to the main records.[62] Going ended his review with warm praise for Church's intellectual strengths for mature minds along with the comment that beginning students are not ready for the book.[63]

> Mr. Church appears to have achieved his declared purpose to approach his subject from an angle and by a method different from any forgoing attempt, and to present a survey of the general structure of cost accounts free from detailed description of any specific system of cost keeping. It is open to question whether the view he gives is "comparatively simple," or indeed whether any simplicity, even comparative, can be given to such a conspectus. Ready comprehension of his subject matter, and even of his diagrams, seems to presuppose a familiarity with the processes of general accounting and the phenomena of manufacturing that comes only after long experience with more elementary aspects. The book is hardly one for student beginners.[64]

Moreover, as the following quote obviously demonstrates, Going held Church in high esteem. An editor himself, Going's near hyperboles of praise for Church's writings takes on even greater meaning. In an article, "The Efficiency Movement: An Outline," Going put Church in some high-flying company.

> Columbus, Vespucci, Balboa, Cabot, Magellan, Hudson—rivals in purpose and in claims—soon proved collectively the nature and delimitations of one and the same new world. So Halsey, Taylor, Emerson, Hine, Pinchot, Talbot, Church—differing in vision and philosophy, differing in space and application of methods—are just beginning to be recognized and to recognize one another as apostles of a single faith—a faith so large, so universal, that it benefits all fields, and in varying guise inhabits all nature animate and inanimate.[65]

R.R. Potter, an engineer writing for the *Engineering News-Record*, emphasized that this book gave the "whys" and "wherefores" for both engineers and bookkeepers. Unlike other reviewers, Potter thought the book was elementary enough for use as a general textbook on accounting and cost keeping for engineers. Apparently, Potter shared Church's view on general accountants. "Incidentally, engineers who have had to cope with the psychology of the accountant at first hand will appreciate Mr. Church's remark that 'the peculiar value of detail to the technical arm has been emphasized with view to exhibit to the general accountant a viewpoint that he sometimes misses.'" Potter also credited Church with developing the machine rate method.[66]

Paul B. Coffman considered "the book to be one of the most scholarly on the subject and thinks it an admirable text for advanced studies in cost accounting."[67] A. van Oss concluded that it was of decided value to students and instructors.[68] Yet, he did cite a failing in Church's text that dealt with Church's supposed carelessness in accounting terminology.

> In passing, the reviewer wants to register his preference for recording payments or accruals of ascertainable rents, taxes, insurance, etc., in accounts called "prepaid" or "accrued" rentals, taxes, etc., rather than using the terms "suspense" or "reserve" to designate their status, fully realizing and admitting that the term "prepaid" is also far from precise. It seems to him better to draw a sharper dividing line between reserves and liabilities also in the terminology.[69]

The writer of this monograph found that Church did add some new discussions in his 1917 work. He did a very nice job on waste, spoilage, scrap, and by-products, a logical extension of his concern for waste of machine capacity. [Idea 21] The accountant has to be as vitally involved in issues of waste, spoilage, scrap, and by-products as he is in accounting for utilization of machinery. Church also added a long discussion of job and production order control system. [Idea 22] Work being performed in the plant must be controlled by a detailed job and production order system. He also was more interested in the timing of expenses. [Idea 23] One must take account of the timing of expenses in passing judgment on management performance for a given period. Church did make a major improvement in tightening his factors of production. [Idea 24] The six factors of production are machinery, organization, supervision, stores transport, power, and space.

By 1917 and even more by 1929, he was being more and more criticized for his carelessness—more likely, it was lack of interest—in bookkeeping and financial accounting matters. Church referred to his view of the "cost man" in the preface of his 1917 book. He made it clear that the "cost man" is not as appreciative of the role of the general accountant as the "cost man" might be. However, he did little more to get at the relationship between the cost accountant and the financial accountant. Since his 1917 book was not very much changed in 1929, Church apparently never developed the much needed synthesis for and empathy with financial accounting. This judgment is slightly softened for his 1930 book, in which he appeared to write from a different frame of reference. This failing was also true with his refusal to go the "journal entry route." One wishes that Church would have been more of a devotee of journal entries, as well as a devotee of the changed terminology of accounting. Maybe by 1917, and definitely in 1929, Church was far removed from the field of accounting.

Church did a better presentation of his machine hour rate system, so much so that his 1917 work represented his best and clearest writing on the subject, even though the "fire" seemed to have been extinguished in the topic. He substituted wavering on the topics of the supplementary rate and the imputation of interest for any further development of his ideas.

1930/1931

Church's 1930 book, *Overhead Expenses: In Relation to Costs, Sales and Profits,* was his last major work in accounting.[70] It was highlighted in the 1931 article, "Overhead: The Cost of Production Preparedness."[71]

Apparently, Church viewed his 1930 book as a more fully expanded version of his 1908 and 1910 books.[72] In fact, he felt the 1930 book was an altogether fresh look at the subject.[73] It was written because Church felt that the attention given to standard costing had caused the topic of overhead to be thrust into the background.[74]

He started the book by stressing that the term "burden" connotes "direct labor as struggling under a heavy load of undeserved misfortune."[75] Church attributed the direct labor approaches of allocation to have been derived from industry out of the habits of the premachinery stage.[76] *"The idea was still to get rid of overhead by plastering it on to production in a then uniform layer."*[77] He stated that overhead is increasing in relation to direct labor and direct materials, but offered no sources or statistical findings to support the "fact."[78] He then posed this problem:

> If it be claimed that we have, let us go a step further. A still more important technical improvement takes place. By enlarging the machine with additional devices, so that it occupies more shop space and uses yet more power, it is made wholly automatic and self-feeding, so that instead of requiring a high-priced operator as at first or a low-priced one as after the original improvement, the machine now requires no operator at all. This means that there are now no more "direct" wages. Is, therefore, the process costing us nothing?[79]

He repeated his philosophy that overhead is not a jumbled mass of expenditures but is comprised of a number of entirely separate services.

> This total cost of all process services is the total cost of running all processes at full time. This is equivalent to the statement that it is the cost of the manufacturing capacity of the plant as a whole. It can also be defined as the total cost of maintaining all the processes of the plant in a state of preparedness for production over a given period, say a week of 48 hours.[80]

Church wished that those who favored the uniform layering of overhead would take a bird's-eye view of a large plant.[81] (You will fully understand this concept after you read Chapter 5 of this monograph.) He excluded from overhead all catastrophic and accidental expenditures[82] and developed a notion of standard working hours.[83] He then formally tied-in his notion of overhead to standard costing. "It follows that not only is standardization of service factors and working hours essential but also that the resulting process cost is a standard cost, in the sense that it is always the same, if the job be done in the same time."[84] The familiar little shop anology works again,[85] and the five factors of production were listed as: (1) space, (2) power, (3) machinery, (4) storage, and (5) transport.[86] He then developed a rent for each factor in the little shop.[87] Church gave a detailed example of determining the amount of the charge for each machine, in which he included: (1) Value of machines, (2) Depreciation, (3) Interest 6%, (4) Repairs, (5) Total, (6) Add Profit 5%, (7) Total Chargeable, and (8) Monthly Amount.[88] This amount was then added as item 3 to the amounts for each machine for (1) Rent, (2) Power, (3) Machinery, so to get (4) Total for month and (5) Hourly Rate, Cents.[89] For more complex shops, two additional factors of superintendence and organization were added.[90] He did mention the 1915 suggestion of Gantt on how to account for idle time. Church remained opposed to Gantt's suggestion on averaging the charge for idle time.[91] However, Church did now agree to the charge to profit and loss.

> ...Finally, the idea that process cost is the cost of capacity to do work enables us to see that its non-utilization does not affect the cost of its capacity but is simply waste that must be met, not by arbitrarily and meaninglessly increasing the cost of work that was actually done but by charging off to profit and loss without permitting it to mix with true cost.[92]

He then gave a farewell blast at the averaging methods and tied his method into budgeting.

> As far as these pages are concerned, the subject of hourly burdens and percentages on wages is finished. In no case do they give more accurate results than the service-factor and process-rate methods. In the great majority of cases they give inaccurate results. While the necessity of budgeting expenditure to provide a basis for service-factor calculations may be considered onerous by some, at least two reasons can be urged in its favor. First that budgeting forces an intimate acquaintance with every detail of the business, and in manufacturing it is mainly the details that spell success or failure. Second, budgeting is being more and more adopted as a wise and necessary precaution, even where it is not being (as it should be) made the basis of the costing system.[93]

Church did add a new way, tool or delivery point, of looking at idle time. *"There is no possible way by which manufacturing profit can be made save by work traveling toward and past the delivery points of production centers.*[94] When work ceases to pass through delivery points, actual loss commences.[95] He then used a new argument, the drip analogy.

> If now material ceases to pass any delivery point, that is, if any particular production center becomes idle, we may picture the process dollar dripping, as it were, uselessly from the delivery point, thus wasting so much supervision, so much cost of maintaining space and machinery and so much of the other service factors concerned.[96]

Church held that standards should be revised any time that any element of direct cost was no longer identical with its corresponding item in the standard cost card.[97] Not surprisingly, he defended his policy in no uncertain terms.

> It may be asked of what value a standard cost is when it is obviously open to revisions of this kind and, in the nature of things, must tend, at any rate eventually, to approach and coincide with actual cost by reason of repeating revisions. The answer is that, so long as it is not made into a fetish, standard cost is a valuable device, because it provided a datum, departures from which can be so tabulated that they reveal the cause of inefficiency by classes.[98]

This writer finds that Church's stand on the accountant versus the production engineer on the issue of standard costs takes an interesting twist that gives the accountant a fairer shake at responsibility and worth.

> This aspect of standard cost does not enter into the scope of this book, for its value lies wholly in the domain of the production engineer and not in that of the accountant. The claim persistently made by some production men that what they term "historical" costing, that is, actual and verifiable record of what did happen, is of no service and that this well-established practice must give way to what are termed "predetermined" costs is due to a complete confusion of terms and to an ignoring of the real purpose of costs.
> So-called "predetermined costs" are not costs at all, but only more or less accurate forecasts. They have their value to production, and, properly handled, it is a very great value, but unless checked and proved by accounting methods there is, as has been shown above, great likelihood of considerable errors being introduced, not only into the cost of jobs incorrectly standardized but also into the cost of correctly standardized ones as well.[99]

Church demanded a detailed collection of actual costs and left the predictions to the production engineer. He also expected a tie-in for internal purposes between the profit on separate jobs and total profit but did not want this information to be disclosed in financial accounting reports, because of all the suppositions that go into the determinations of profit by jobs.[100]

Furthermore, Church no longer mandated a separate hourly rate for each production center, although he realized that it was necessary sometimes.[101] The notion of "rent" was used to explain his overhead allocation philosophy. "In other words, expenditures are standardized *over a sufficiently long period* to absorb local irregularities."[102] In short, the goal of the philosophy was this:

> What has been done here is, in fact, the carrying out of departmentalization as far as the individual production center. As departments must have homogeneous processing to enable a single process rate to be applied to their work, in the present case we have narrowed down the application of service factors so that each machine or production center can carry on an individual type of processing and yet be costed with equal precision. But, as remarked above, this final refinement is unnecessary so long as we can divide up manufacturing operations into departments of homogeneous processing. It is only when it becomes necessary to include in one department several types of production center or varieties of product which are not all processed alike that the hourly process rate must be worked out for each such center.[103]

Note that Church's basic theme had not changed in 1930 from 1901. He was still fighting against the same formidable enemy—the vagueness of overhead.

> But this computation is not merely that of a vague expenditure known as "overhead." The division of all expenditure into service factors enables the scrutiny to become far more precise than it would be if merely an assembly of annual expenditures in a general way were in question. It enables the mind to form a clear picture of different classes of activity, because expenditures are seen in groups and in relation to the ends to be effected. In tabulating the expenditure of the power factor, or of the supervision factor, or of the storekeeping-transport factor, the essential or necessary character of this or the other item of expenditure is easily reviewed. Consequently, when some hundreds of items are assembled in perhaps seven or eight factors, though an item here or there may have been misjudged, the final result should be very close to actual figures, provided conditions are unchanged.[104]

He, however, broke with his past accounting writings and sent the cost of superfluous service to profit and loss and not to the cost of the product.[105] The supplementary cost was to be used as only a memorandum or indicator of utilization.[106] He offered a lament on this topic later on in his book.

> ...At the time in question, nearly twenty years ago, the idea of separating wasted capacity (idle time) from true cost of jobs was entirely new and unfamiliar. No other method than that of percentages, and, to a small degree, hourly burdens, was in use, and, in introducing the new views on overhead, it was desirable not to depart too far from established usage, which, of course, called for the prorating of all current expenditure over current jobs. By the device of the waste ratio, or as it was termed the "supplementary rate," this complete prorating was still possible, although the author was careful to point out that it was not essential, and that the waste ratio was not and could not be part of true cost.
>
> As it turned out, no element of the new method was more severely criticized than the "supplementary rate." It was (somewhat to the author's surprise) generally recognized that it was no part of true cost and that, therefore, wasted capacity should be charged off to profit and loss. Today, this idea is so generally accepted that there is perhaps no danger in the contrary course. But at the time of the original publication of the method, this was by no means the case, and the dangers were perhaps too much emphasized by the writer.[107]

In the same manner, Church seemed to view "overtime" as less of an evil than before and, in fact, seemed to treat it as a friend, as overtime meant that fixed overhead was to be spread over more working hours.[108] A rigorous definition was given for overhead items that should be charged directly to profit and loss. They were "exceptional, irregular, or even catastrophic in nature."[109] He ended with this clear statement of why these items should be charged to profit and loss.

> In all cases of this kind, where an alternative exists between so treating an item that it will find its way into costs and so treating it that it is met out of profits, it is better, provided it is not a recurrent expenditure of any kind, to write it off either at once or by degrees without letting it enter overhead, that is, any one factor. Increasing cost means putting a handicap on competitive power, so that in the end less profits will be made and less available for any purpose, including the writing off in question. If an obstacle is met and an expenditure of some amount can clear that obstacle from the normal manufacturing operations, and if then this amount is written off out of profits, the productive forces are put on the same footing as though the obstacle had not existed at all. And as it is possible that competitors will have met with no such obstacle, the firm is putting itself back on the same footing as its competitors. Under such conditions it would seem advisable to meet the enhanced cost out of profits, if possible.[110]

Church also came to grips with departmentalization and the service factors.

> ...As far as costs are concerned, departmentalization is merely a device for the much easier collection and the closer control over items. By narrowing down the assembly of service-factor charges to individual departments, they take on a much more concrete and practically controllable form.[111]

He was quite willing to combine the direct labor cost in a process with the overhead costs to get an overall process rate.[112] Church remained against the notion of averaging the costs of new property with the costs of old property.[113] He favored a combined interest and depreciation rate, so to arrive at a constant amount for the total charges of interest and depreciation through the years,[114] and also favored keeping cost accounting records free of revaluations of property.

> While there is no objection to revaluations of this kind and the setting up of reserves, etc., on the books in accordance with the difference between the true and the supposed values, such modifications should not be allowed to enter the detailed accounts. Capital value for the purposes of cost accounting should be the value at which the equipment was purchased. To tamper with this quite definite figure would very soon lead to an accounting erection build on shifting sand, so that after few alterations of this kind the precise significance of the figures yielded by the accounts would be exceedingly difficult to determine and still more difficult to compare on any intelligible basis with those of other years.[115]

As you will see in Chapter 6, Church was much concerned in the 1920's about questions of storage and transport. He felt that the allocation of the storage-transport factor should not be based on the value of the material but on the value and importance of machinery in the processing center.[116] In any event, the allocation of the storage-transport factor is not as easy as square footage for space or kilowatt hours for power, but a satisfactory result can be accomplished by use of careful judgment.[117] The number of delivery points would be a good method of allocating the costs of the supervision factor.[118] The organization factor is the most difficult to allocate.[119] He then summarized these factors into a process rate: (1) Space, (2) Power, (3) Storage-Transport, (4) Supervision, (5) Organization, (6) Productive Equipment, (7) Special, and (8) Operative Labor (if included).[120]

Church saved his last defense for those who misunderstood the importance of the imputation of interest topic. The apologetic tone found in the supplementary rate issue defense is not present here. Church is far from repentant.

> The objection to the inclusion of interest on equipment in costs comes usually from accountants whose comprehension of overhead and its real place in relation to cost is limited to the old vague mathematical relationships—ratios and hourly burdens. Seeing overhead as a mass of figures having no ascertainable relation to the only things that they were able to determine with precision, namely, direct labor and direct material (or that used to be called "flat cost" or "prime cost"), it is not surprising that the utility of including an additional item in the jumbled mass was not very apparent. It was, in fact, almost entirely useless under the older methods of costing. But when interest is allowed to act as the natural measure of the use of capital in production, the matter takes on another aspect. While service factors and process rates can be set up without including capital charges, to do so would be to falsify them under normal conditions, and, therefore, render them much less reliable as measures of the relative as well as the absolute cost of processing than is otherwise the case.[121]

As you will notice in the review of his 1923 book in Chapter 5, Church had not given up on the allocation and control of selling expenses. While he considered selling expenses much less amenable to standardization than manufacturing capacity, allocations would be made to classes of product.[122]

Church immediately followed the 1930 book with an article, "Overhead—The Cost of Production Preparedness," in January, 1931.[123] The abstract for the article refers to the struggle over overhead allocation. "Every new use of automated equipment increases the importance of a correct distribution of overhead. Yet industry keeps on striking a meaningless ratio between burden and cost which clouds the picture of the effectiveness of overhead expenditures or their impingement upon processes. Legitimate overhead is no part of the cost of the product. It is the cost of production preparedness."[124] He remained as flamboyant as ever in describing the popular methods of allocation. "...Although a ratio has been struck, it is both accidental and temporary. Nothing has resulted but an arbitrary and misleading mathematical trick."[125] Church recognized that his definition of overhead, as depicted in his 1901/1908 and 1909/1910 works, had some short-comings, but he convincingly reaffirmed that, as theory, it made sense, and in terms of practical usage, was a "forward step" that led to an efficient working methodology.

> In two books published some years ago, I developed the principle that overhead is merely a collective term for several distinct and separate services, each of which has its separate incidence on production, and that it is possible to waste these services as well as to utilize them for actual production. Although this separation of factors which had formerly been lumped into a total was put forward as a practical method of cost-finding rather than as a formal theory, it was a forward step. It has led to the further inference, not then developed, that overhead is not the cost of product, but of something else. That something is preparedness.[126]

Church then attempted to explain his overhead control philosophy based on four efficiencies of production. They were: "(1) The efficiency of preparedness—how does the actual compare with the necessary cost of maintaining a capacity?; (2) The efficiency of utilization—how much of the normal capacity is utilized?; (3) The efficiency of processing time—is each job done in the shortest possible time; and (4) The efficiency of direct labor—are wage costs too high relatively to process cost?"[127] Because a correlation might not have been readily apparent, Church described the tie-in between items (3) and (4).

> The reason why high wages are frequently more economical than lower rates may be inferred if we examine the interplay of processing time, process-rate cost and direct-wage cost. The higher the process rate, the more we can afford to pay out for incentive to reduce processing time. Even though the cost of direct wages per unit of product does not diminish, there will often be an important saving in process-rate cost and therefore in total cost.[128]

Church's goal, then, was to free capacity. He stressed that a wage incentive plan might appear to be cost ineffective if a percentage or hourly labor burden method were used but in reality would have been good because of capacity freed for other jobs.[129]

Garner noted Church's capitulation in 1930 on the issue of using the profit and loss statement for loss due to idle capacity.[130] Brummet did also.[131] Coffman thought the book to be an elaboration of the 1901/1908 and 1909/1910 efforts.[132] Thorton thought Church was in line with "the attempt to convert indirect to directly measurable costs by metering and measuring is rapidly gaining ground."[133] He concluded "No work by A. Hamilton Church should be omitted from the library of the cost accountant. This book is the most important and the best work on cost accounting that your reviewer knows."[134]

The writer of this monograph considered that Church posed an interesting query to those who used direct labor approaches to overhead allocation. [Idea 25] What happens when the last direct laborer is gone from the plant? He did a fairly nice job discussing the exclusion of catastrophic and accidental items from overhead. [Idea 26] All catastrophies and accidental items should be excluded from overhead. Budgeting had come of age. [Idea 27] Budgeting mandated the service-factor calculations. Church finally did much more with standard costing than in his previous writings. [Idea 28] Standards should be changed whenever any element of direct cost is no longer identical with its corresponding item in the standard cost card. [Idea 29] Standards must be checked against actual accounting data. He did seem to be a little more concerned with financial accounting. [Idea 30] While management must know the profit from each job, they should not disclose this in financial accounting reports because of the many suppositions going into this profit calculation. [Idea 31] Revaluations of property for financial accounting purposes should not be given effect in the cost accounting records because of internal comparison purposes.

Church continued with the tie-in of accounting with the internal operations of the organization. [Idea 32] Direct labor might be merged with overhead costs to get a single processing rate. [Idea 33] A constant amount of a total of depreciation and interest provides the best figure for cost planning purposes. [Idea 34] It is possible to find a rational basis for allocating factors such as storage-transport, supervision, and organization.

Perhaps the 1930 book should best be viewed not as an elaboration or a more fully expanded version but as an apology (in the classic sense) for his 1901/1908 and 1909/1910 works. Church was 64 years old when the book was published and probably wanted to fit his life's efforts into such newer concepts as standard costing, departmentalization, budgeting, cost estimating, and, possibly, direct costing. He probably wanted to clear the decks of the supplementary rate debacle and he did. He held firm on the imputation of interest and even added a profit amount to his factor cost computation. While never really discussing the financial accounting implications, he did handle such issues as catastrophic and accidental expenses to profit and loss, revaluations, loss due to idle time, and profits by jobs in a manner that showed just a little more empathy to financial accounting than his other writings.

As well as the book is written, it is still far from his most meaningful contribution. It fits in well with his efforts but he seemed to have lost his fervor about his major ideas of the machine hour rate method and production centers. A person reading only the 1930 book would probably tend to slight these ideas. That would be tragic.

1934

As previously mentioned, the writer attributed the section "Machine Hour Rate" in L. P. Alford's *Cost and Production Handbook* to Church, who was listed as a contributing editor to that book.[135] This section showed an overview of the status in 1934 of Church's idea. For instance, the machine-hour rate could be used "(a) as an inclusive single rate, absorbing all of the burden and also all of the direct labor cost as well; (b) as an exclusive single rate, absorbing all of the burden, but with direct labor cost charged separately; (c) as a supplementary or 'super' rate used in conjunction with another rate or other rates based upon direct labor hours or some other factor."[136]

The machine hour rate concept had been well received by then. The Joint Committee on Management Terminology had a definition for it.[137] The writer of the section noted that "perhaps interest on value of the equipment used" was to be included as a cost in the machine rate determination.[138] Apparently, some compromise on the complexity issue had been reached.

> In *arranging machine classes and rates*, it is not necessary that a rate be established for each individual machine, and it is not necessary that machines in the same class be continuous. In fact, it is sometimes possible to group small inexpensive machines of even different types providing they have the same approximate size, initial cost, and maintenance cost.[139]

There must have been adoptions of the machine-hour rate method by some industry groups. References were made to statements of accounting policy from the Drop Forging Institute, the Millwork Cost Bureau, and the Pressed Metal Institute.[140]

The writer of this monograph is not able to prove the first attribution but common sense applied to a study of the various sections of the *Handbook* would probably result in most of the readers agreeing with that attribution. This is not so true with the second attribution of "Manufacturing or Production Orders."[141] The writer of that section did quote from Church in his 1929 book.[142] Certainly, he was very interested in the topic. Since the section was not theoretical and covered a relatively non-controversial area, it is not reviewed in this monograph.

The writer of this monograph considers that the possible use of the machine-hour rate approach as a "super rate" is a new idea for Church. [Idea 35] Management may use the machine hour rate concept as a "super rate" to analyze its current allocation method and its operating efficiency. Obviously, it is unfortunate to end the review of his writing in accounting with two attributed writings but it also would have been unfortunate not to note Church in the list of contributing editors of Alford's work. Fifty years have destroyed all evidence of Church's role in the 1934 *Handbook*.

CHAPTER FIVE
MANAGEMENT WRITINGS

The following management writings cover three decades and various aspects of management ranging from the level of the foreman to the chief executive. They are grouped into five time periods: 1900; 1911 and 1912; 1913 and 1914; 1915; and 1923. The format for the chapter will be the same as in chapters 3 and 4.

1900

Church's first article, "The Meaning of Commercial Organization," appeared in *The Engineering Magazine* in December of 1900. It was, most likely, considered to be a continuation, if not a conclusion, of a series of articles written by J. Slater Lewis, who was quite ill at the time[1] and who died in July of 1901.[2] The editorial comment with the article was along those lines. "Mr. Church, the associate of Mr. J. Slater Lewis, is one of the leaders of the new science of modern manufacturing. The strong feature of his article is his demonstration that organization is an integral and even basal part of successful works management—not merely an auxiliary to it."[3]

Church started with the theme that was to continue throughout his writings—the manufacturing world had entered an extremely more complex arena.[4] "The spectacle afforded by a modern works of the first grade is one of a great series of independent operations, carried on out of sight and for the most part out of knowledge of one another, but so carefully and cunningly devised that their products are in perfect coordination."[5] "...Close on the heels of the machine tool came the necessity for an altogether higher type of intelligence to control the increasing complexity of industrial operations. The 'mechanic' disappears; in his place we have the 'captain' of industry..."[6]

The nerve analogy was used to explain the coordination needed for control; accounting was just one of these factors.

> From a practical point of view it may be said that as coordination is the imperative of today; the nerve system must be rearranged with that end kept steadily in view. The object of the commercial, or, as it might also be termed, the administrative organization scheme, should be to collect knowledge of what is going forward, not merely qualitatively, but quantitatively; it should also provide the means of regulating as well as the means of recording. It is no mere matter of accountancy, although the element of cost is an important factor. Nor is the matter merely a technical one. It is essentially a matter of administrative control that is in question, stretching through every department and regulating the healthy life of the whole.[7]

Church started out early with his ambivalent, and sometimes caustic, views towards book-keeping and accounting. "Epigrammatically it may be said that there is some bookkeeping in organization, but that there is no organization in bookkeeping."[8] Continuing in this vein of criticism, Church wrote:

> More especially must it be emphasized that a knowledge of what is termed prime cost is no evidence of an intelligent control of the commercial side of a manufacturing busi-ness... The analysis of the working indirect expenses of the business, and in particular the discrimination between "works expense"—that is, the expenditure on productive departments—and "general establishment expenditure"—representing the expenses of the selling organization—is a principle the fundamental importance of which had only dimly been realized by the book-keeping mind, and was first given the prominence due to its importance in the Slater Lewis system.[9]

Applying the nerve analogy still further, Church promoted that central control replace "the master's eyes and brain in the daily progress of his work."[10] According to Church, this was best achieved in a centralized and mechanized accounting department.[11] Holding no na-tional bias, Church contrasted the "go-ahead United States"[12] attitude of progress with the stagnant state of Great Britain, where energies were being wasted on "learned professions" and amateur politicians.[13]

Church also took the opportunity in his first work to express his concerns as to why a con-trol system had to be complex. This concern brought up the theme of increased competition—an obvious essential to the realization of effective cost control.

> With the growth of competition the necessity for co-ordination and of an accurate and swift presentation of results is more and more imperative. The margin for waste is less, the necessity for detail greater. Everything should be the subject of forecast as to financial results, and of prearrangements as to the actual carrying out. And when it is completed, the records of what did actually take place should be capable of comparison with what was intended to take place. Control then becomes a living reality. Co-ordination implies prevision of neces-sity. The place where it pays to spend time and money on work is before it has begun the serious and irrecoverable expenses of production. It is the place, too, where it is most effi-ciently applied to produce a maximum of smooth working.[14]

Generally, the ideas offered in this article were principles which need to be applied to "the diversity of the local needs of each special business."[15] The article ended with a strong call for accounting control.

> With these arrangements should be coupled—in all businesses in which orders have an individuality, e.g., machinery—a method of finding not only the total works cost, including charges, but also the expenses incurred by the individual order after sale, such as commis-sions, freight, customs duty, workman's out-time and travelling expenses, and the like. The difference between the aggregate of these sums and the sale price is the net profit on that transaction. The sum of all such profits in any period should agree with the profit as declared by the financial books. Every item of profit, as well as every item of loss should be traceable by the management, and no covering up allowed. If these elements are established and intelligently made use of, we have as near approach to the restoration of personal control over the details of a large business as the situation permits.[16]

In his review of Church's first work, Litterer stated that Church focused on the conditions of internal confusion and disorder which apparently marked the era of the 1890's.[17] There was a need for a managerial solution and for top-notch people in management.[18] Although Jelinek relied heavily on Litterer's work for her review of Church,[19] she spent much more time than Litterer did focusing on the control feature, as described by Church. Jelinek wrote, "By restoring control 'in its essential features', however, Church clearly meant something more than controlling minute details. He is focusing not on the details, but on how they fit together."[20]

The writer of this monograph holds that Church early on developed central themes for his management writings. There is some overlap between the two areas of accounting and management but he tended not to be redundant, although this may have been carried to the extreme and prevented an holistic view of his works. These themes are first treated in the idea format. Church wrote of the excitement of the 1890's. Since this time marked the beginnings of the new field of study of management, it must have been as exciting as Church felt it to be. [Idea 36] The manufacturing world has entered an extremely more complex arena. This called for control. [Idea 37] The control system for an organization is as needed as and similar in function to the nervous system of a person. [Idea 38] The control system must replace the master's eyes and brains in the daily progress of work. [Idea 39] The increasing threat of competition has caused the need for complex control systems to coordinate the many parts of the organization.

The next theme, as stated in Idea 40, was to be repeated time and time again. It became, later on, a prime thrust in the war that was to break out between Church and the disciples of Taylor. [Idea 40] Each business is different, and local needs must be met within the framework of overall principles. The theme of Idea 41 is closely related to accounting—or more specifically—to the accountant. The next two ideas enumerate other necessities of accounting. [Idea 41] Prime costs are not enough to know. [Idea 42] The accounting staff should be in a centralized location. [Idea 43] A continuous stock-taking system is necessary to arrive at the needed accounting statements.

The last theme for this section is more difficult to list in the idea format, in that it deals with the very qualitative judgement of which country is the leading country in manufacturing. Church had no doubt. He expressed this in 1900 and many other times later. [Idea 44] The United States is where to look for progress in manufacturing.

It should be clear that any final interpretations of Church's writings in accounting can not be made without a review of all his efforts. This is true for each one of the four areas in which he wrote; especially since his efforts in the business and society area and in the industrial engineering area have apparently not been reviewed at all. For instance, the 1900 writing did not contain the specifics of control that his 1901 writings did. While Jelinek stressed the need for general control as a key feature of Church's 1900 writing, she did not stress Church's concern with control at the detail level as well.

It is also clear that Church in his first management writing showed the same lack of empathy for bookkeeping/accounting. There was such a thing as a "bookkeeping mind" but it was never defined. It is probable that this reference was to the notion that a bookkeeper was more interested in recording the event in the broadest possible context—i.e., with as few accounts as possible—and not aware of, or interested in, the potential managerial uses of data. By now, the reader is familiar with Church's use of the bookkeeper/accountant as a strawman. However, while he was not explicit about the shortcomings of the mentality of the bookkeeper/accountant, there were more definite statements about the desired organization of the bookkeeping and accounting staff—and in its output, statements each month.

1911 and 1912

By 1911 Church appeared to have shifted some of his attention from the field of manufacturing accounting to manufacturing management. His 1911 articles laid the groundwork for his epically important and pivotal collaboration with Alford in 1912, on which he further elaborated at the 1912 ASME (American Society of Mechanical Engineers) meeting in New York at the discussion of the report of its Subcommittee on Administration. There were 2 articles in 1911 and 1 in 1912, not including the comments at the 1912 meeting. It is important to note that his discussion at the 1912 meeting has not been previously listed by other reviewers of Church.

Church published his cornerstone article "The Meaning of Scientific Management" in the April, 1911 issue of *The Engineering Magazine*.[21] This article led to the 1912 collaboration with

Alford and the author received quite a favorable review by the editors, as noted in Chapter 2.[22]

There was no magic formula for introducing "scientific management," since it represented the works and writings of many for decades. As Church himself observed: "The evolution of this body of principles was bound to take place because it was called for by the necessities of modern industry."[23] He then proceeded to clarify why scientific management is a "way of looking at the whole problem of industrial production," as a body of principles rather than as a system.

> It cannot be too clearly emphasized that scientific management is a body of principles and not a "system". These principles may be applied in a great variety of ways, so long as the basic ideas are not departed from. It is not a particular style or method of organization, or a particular way of laying out a shop, or of keeping stores and raw materials—still less has it any relation to a particular set of forms, cards or books. It is a particular way of looking at the whole problem of industrial production, and nothing beyond.[24]

Church warned that "scientific management," while bringing the "human" element of management into play, has not settled the warring claims of capital and labor.[25] He then gave an example in a drafting department of his first basic principle—the planning of industrial activity from a consideration of its simplest units. His second basic principle was the comparing of actual results with the forecast *possible maximum* of results and thus determining the ratio of efficiency.[26] Some of these catchy sentences can only be savored by direct quotes.

> The moral effect of it, in addition to the tuning up of all departments, is the raising all round of the average perception of accuracy of observation and of performance—accuracy, and ever more accuracy.
> In brief, it is the application of accurate thinking, accurate planning, and accurate doing, so as to increase output, reduce cost, and by consequence render available a larger margin of surplus for division between employer and employee.[27]
> It is possible that this may have an influence on the more thoughtful type of workman, by leading him to realise how wide from the facts are the claims of Socialism that labour is the creator of all wealth...[28]
> Even in the most backward plant every change should be evolutionary—starting from what exists and developing it towards a higher state of efficiency. Root-and-branch changes are rarely satisfactory. When it is realised that true scientific management does not mean pulling everything up by the roots, but is largely a matter of tuning up to concert pitch of the existing organization, and then the gradual introduction of accurate planning—always with an eye to the expense account—then it may encourage some who are now trembling on the brink.[29]
> ...Generally speaking, the formulation of principles of building up from unit operation, and of determining a possible maximum of work as "efficiency" and any failure to realise this standard as waste, will rank as one of the epoch-making events in the history of the mechanical arts...[30]

Clearly, Church felt that the shop foreman had an integral role to play in an intensive production setting. He wrote of the dangers of bypassing the shop foreman in the process of systemization in the "Intensive Production and the Foreman,"[31] published in 1911.

> In certain quarters there is a tendency to systematize the foreman out of existence altogether. This is most popular with the "root and branch" reformers who insist that efficiency can only be reached by yielding control of a plant for an indefinite period to experts trained in a particular school. Personally I must confess to a certain amount of skepticism as to the necessity for such autocratic introduction of reforms, and still greater skepticism as to the permanence of the efficiency obtained in that way. But as very few owners will be found who do not prefer to trust to evolutionary rather than revolutionary methods, I shall deal here only with the question of plants that are feeling their way toward efficiency by healthy and gradual progress.[32]

The foreman's role, therefore, should be redefined in this new world so to "preserve his usefulness and protect him from the inroads of reformers who have only a vague idea of what he is there for."[33]

> The whole idea of having a foreman is a delegation of control for certain purposes. Chief among those purposes is the maintenance of a certain elasticity, which will take up lost motion and compensate for the machine-like character of even the best organization by subdividing the general supervision into sections small enough for all the current events in each of them to be grasped by the foreman concerned.[34]

The foreman "...represents the last outpost of general control as distinguished from special control"[35] and "represents the master's eyes in the department over which he is set."[36] Church felt that the foreman would now be more involved with observations to be sure that what the specialists recommend makes sense within his department.[37]

The heralded article, "The Principles of Management," written with Alford, was published in the May 30, 1912 issue of the *American Machinist*. The writers were interested in developing the skeleton of a real scientific art of management rather than in focusing attention on any one special system.[38] Their three principles were:

> (1) the systematic use of experience;
> (2) the economic control of effort; and
> (3) the promotion of personal effectiveness.[39]

The systematic use of experience is ..."the careful analysis of what is about to be attempted, and its reference to existing records and standards of performance."[40] The economic control of effort had five parts:

> (1) division of effort;
> (2) co-ordination of effort;
> (3) conservation of effort;
> (4) remuneration of effort; and
> (5) the function of comparison.[41]

The promotion of personal effectiveness was not tightly defined. It was based on a "square deal" in the course of relations during working hours.[42] *Espirit de corps* was stressed, as well as physical surroundings and leadership.[43]

> Of all the conditions controlling a fine working atmosphere, leadership probably plays the most important part. In warfare men prefer to serve under the general who wins battles, though that entails hardships without number and toil without end. In industrialism, mechanism is a mighty important thing compared with an "old man" who is a born leader of men.[44]

Church devoted much more attention to these principles in his 1914 book, and, as such, a more detailed review of them is given later on in this chapter. He and Alford, however, used this article to attack the various schools of scientific management. The writers warned against pushing management principles to their limits, as the limiting conditions were not yet formulated.[45]

> By many of the enthusiastic advocates of particular systems of management, the existence of limiting conditions is hardly suspected, consequently they ride their favorite hobby to exhaustion, till many useful ideas become discredited in the eyes of practical men. It is not enough to know that a principle can be applied; it is even more important to know when not to apply it.[46]

Both Church and Alford were of the opinion that the Taylorites fell into this category of enthusiastic but misguided advocates of a system, invalidated by its lack of boundaries. The writers threw down the gauntlet to the Taylorites. "...Mr. Taylor's 'scientific management' is a collection of axioms and an arbitrary combination of specific mechanisms rather than a body of principles. Among its leading features, time study, functional foremanship, standardization, planning in advance, and task-bonus may be selected as characteristics."[47] They continued: "One more point of Taylor's system may be mentioned. It is his claim that the science which underlies each act of each workman is able to fully understand it (and presuma-

59

bly give it effect) without specific and very detailed guidance from above."[48] Church and Alford quickly analyzed and dismissed the twelve principles written by Harrington Emerson.[49] The writers were by no means modest about their effort.

> The important point is, of course, that by stating and fixing what are believed to be the three basic and fundamental principles of industrial activity, and deriving the subordinate details from these in logical order, a beginning has been made toward finding a truly scientific basis for the art of management, on which all its prime facts can be built up, later, into a coherent and understandable system of theory and practice.[50]

Alford was a member and the secretary of the ASME subcommittee on Administration,[51] which presented its majority report "The Present State of the Art of Industrial Management"[52] in New York in December of 1912.[53] The subcommittee endorsed Church and Alford's principles, in addition to adding another principle of the transference of skill.

> We have pointed out that the underlying principle, that is, cause in the widest sense, the application of which has built up modern industry, is the transference of skill. This basic principle is put into effect on the management side of all industrial activities, through three regulative principles which sum up the ideas in the above quotations, Pars, 39 and 40. These have been concisely stated as: (a) the systematic use of experience; (b) the economic control of effort; (c) the promotion of personal effectiveness.[54]

Church was at the presentation of the report and was the third of 25 persons, over a five hour period, to discuss it.[55] In this response, Church connected the transference of skill issue to the importance of machines issue.

> The more I think over this problem, the more I am convinced that the true line of progress is the exhaustive study of machines, their capacities and limitations. I have held this opinion for many years, and the system of industrial accounting I have been advocating for the past decade was, I believe, the first step made towards bringing forward the machine to its true place as a factor of production. But I must confess that until this principle of the transference of skill was brought out so clearly by this report, I did not realize exactly why the machine tool was frequently so surprisingly ineffective under indifferent handling.[56]

Church also pointed out that the subcommittee had adopted his and Alford's three principles of management model.[57] The habit stage is crucial, he said, because the right kind and degree of habit by every person involved in production should be created.[58]

> It is not enough for the workman to be so instructed that he forms good habit. Every living link in the chain of production requires equally to be so trained that his acquired habit is harmonious with all the rest. The report has mentioned this aspect of the question where it insists that the executives and not the workman are the persons most important to be reached. Few people understand that the principal work of an expert organizer is not the designing of elaborate blanks and cards, but the fostering, with tireless patience, of correctly adjusted habit in each member of the staff.[59]

Once again the rhetorically-minded Church enhanced his argument with an articulate analogy about the state of management at that time.

> Scientific men tell us that the great difference between a savage race and a highly civilized one is that the former remains in a condition of natural innocence, and the latter has arrived at self-consciousness. This, I think, is the real state of affairs in regard to management engineering. We are passing from a stage at which there was a simple and unconscious following of tradition, into a stage of self-consciousness in which we are moved to subject our habits and our motives to severe self-scrutiny, and examine afresh every item of our daily practice. It is a very painful stage to have arrived at. Most of us are so content with our comfortable natural innocence that we do not like to part with it, but it is a process that once commenced, must continue.[60]

As would be expected, Church's comments were interpreted as being directed at Taylor. Carl Barth rose at the conference session to defend Taylor and Taylorism against what he viewed as an attack by Church. Barth claimed that Taylor had not neglected the study of machines but that he had done so 25 years earlier when he first studied the art of cutting metals.[61]

Kimball responded almost immediately to the May 30, 1912 article.[62] He felt that nearly all people interested in shop management would be in hardy accord with the spirit of the article.[63] He wrote that the article had cleared away the underbrush and was an outgrowth of Taylor's works.[64] Calder, in the same issue as Kimball, feared that slavish insistence upon one "system of detail which takes no account of the variety of industrial conditions and problems" threatened the arduous labor of Taylor.[65] Calder wrote that Church and Alford's article deserved and will receive careful attention from progressive engineers and production managers.[66]

Merrill chose the May 30, 1912 article as one of his classic articles in management.[67] He classified Church and Alford as being in a group of critics of Taylor because of his failure to arrive at principles of management.[68] Church and Alford wanted to go deeper.[69] "Their comments on the frequent lack of relationship between physical working conditions and morale provide a foretaste of Mayo's conclusions," Merrill claimed.[70]

Wren devoted a few pages to Alford and to Church in The Evolution of Management Thought,[71] writing that because Alford and Church stressed the weakness of the Taylor approach, they paved the way for broader, more accurate principles of management. As Wren describes it, Alford and Church thought the Taylor approach "superseded the art of leadership by substituting an elaborate mechanism or system. This did not mean that the mechanism was useless, but rather that it overlooked the dynamic possibilities of effective leadership. Alford thought that Taylor's so-called 'principles' were too mechanical, and to remedy this he (and Church) proposed three broad principles....From these three broad regulative principles, a truly scientific basis for the art of management could be discovered."[72]

In his review of Church's 1911 article from The Engineering Magazine, Litterer said that Church more adequately explained the reasons why activities such as routing, dispatching, and other production control components were service activities subordinate to the principle of management.[73] In a review with a similar bent, Jelinek posed this insight.

> ...Church and Alford obviously sought to go far beyond Taylor in generality, however. Their "experience" principle is equally applicable to routine and to new situations, particularly where analytic thinking may be used, much as Taylor himself advocated the use of elemental actions to build a sequential estimate of a new job, or as Gilbreth sought "therbligs." In addition, the principle enunciated by Church and Alford is applicable at higher levels of logic; it is not limited to the concrete details of oiling a machine, laying bricks, or even constructing a time-keeping system. They suggest that it is applicable to systems of management as well.[74]

The writer of this monograph found that there were three sets of ideas in this section. The first set came from the April, 1911 article and stressed more global matters. [Idea 45] Scientific Management is a body of principles and not a system. These principles may be applied in a great variety of ways, as long as the principles are kept. [Idea 46] Scientific Management has not settled the warring claims of capital and labor. [Idea 47] The following of the principles of management will lead to a greater pot to be shared by employees. [Idea 48] Labor is not the creator of all wealth. [Idea 49] Change should be evolutionary, not revolutionary.

Church again showed his ability to be concerned with both global matters in the preceding article and detailed matters in the foremanship article in the American Machinist. The second set of ideas in this section comes from the latter article. [Idea 50] The role of the foreman is to provide elasticity of reactions to current events within the rigidity of the organization. [Idea 51] The foreman represents the last outpost of general control and is the master's eyes for that department.

The third set of ideas came from his 1912 efforts and center around his and Alford's principles of management.[Idea 52] The three principles of management are: (1) The systematic use of experience; (2) the economic control of effort; and (3) the promotion of personal effectiveness. [Idea 53] The systematic use of experience is the careful analysis of what is about to be attempted, and its reference to existing records and standards of performance. [Idea 54] A "square deal" is needed for workers. [Idea 55] Leadership is probably the most important part of a fine work atmosphere. [Idea 56] Good work habits should be created for all.

Church was apparently a democratic friend of the people and in favor of local initiative in the work place. He held high hopes for the future of workers and their well being and their ability to see through socialism. Every worker was important to Church.

It is hard to recreate the controversies of 70 to 80 years ago surrounding "scientific management" and the back-biting that went on between Taylor, his disciples, and opponents like Church and Alford. However, it is probably safe to conclude that Church would have been accused of raising a red herring in his 1911 article in *The Engineering Magazine*. He apparently used the strawman approach again and this time the "systemizers" were the bundled straw. They were so interested in forms, cards, and books that they could only try to repeat their performances even in a very different setting. He again argued for the uniqueness of the employment of these techniques of management.

But there were general principles of management which transcended forms, cards, and books. In 1911 Church claimed two general principles; by 1912, he and Alford arrived at three. They skillfully avoided a series of rigid laws derived from these principles. Since Alford later turned to the "laws of management approach", as witnessed in his 1928 book *Laws of Management Applied to Manufacturing*,[75] Church must be given much credit for the general nature of the 1912 writing.

The stage has now been set for some monumental efforts by Church in 1913 and 1923 in the field of management. He was ready for this take-off. He had a strong and varied background in various businesses. He had worked with some of the greats. He had been an outstanding success in the field of cost accounting with such well recognized innovations as the machine-hour rate method and production centers. He was obviously well read. He had strong writing and editorial abilities and contacts. He was sold on America. He had a healthy respect for his talents and was very willing to propagandize his efforts. He clearly was willing to engage in combat. His strawmen were set-up and ready to knock down.

1913 and 1914

In 1913 Church published a six article series entitled "Practical Principles of Rational Management" in *The Engineering Magazine*.[76] These articles were rewritten and published as Church's seminal work in management, *The Science and Practice of Management* in 1914.[77] This monograph reviews the 1914 book and not the 1913 articles. The book was preceded by a summary of it in two articles in *The Efficiency Journal* of February, 1914.[78] These articles are not reviewed here.

The 1914 book had 394 pages of text and five additional shorter texts in the appendix. Two of the shorter texts are reviewed in the monograph. Two of the three shorter texts not reviewed were copies of two articles which will be reviewed in Chapter Six. The third short text, "Some Axioms of Administration," was a blend of many of his shorter articles and not a good blend at that. Hence, it is not reviewed.

The writer often recalls a statement he heard some time ago. It was as one grows older (and, hopefully, wiser), he no longer skips the author's preface and runs to the text, but instead studies the preface in great depth. This writer was pleased to find that this recollection paid off when reading Church's preface to the 1914 book. Church revealed his personal evolution from accountant to manager in transparent terms. He wrote that his earlier work focused on accounting for the various factors of manufacturing, whereas this work attempted to formulate a true science of management.

The method therein applied has now been used in an analysis of the facts of manufacturing administration. It has been endeavored to ascertain the fundamental facts of production, not from the viewpoint of costs, but from the viewpoint of management. Instead of trying to throw light on the nature of expense, I have endeavored to throw light on the nature of organization. In other words, this book is an attempt to formulate such fundamental facts and such fundamental regulative principles as may be hereafter developed into a true science of management.[79]

Church praised Taylor and Harrington Emerson but again expressed concern about their imitators.

The question of formulating some approach to a true science of management has been in the air for some time. The first and most forceful stirring of the subject is unquestionably due to Mr. Frederick W. Taylor, whose paper on "Shop Management," issued in 1903, opened most persons' eyes to the fact that administration was ceasing to be an empirical thing—a kind of trade secret, known only to a few men—and that it was entering a stage where things could be reasoned about instead of being guessed at. Later on Mr. Harrington Emerson emphasized the human element in the problem—the mental qualifications necessary to efficiency. Unfortunately, the useful tendency thus initiated soon led to unforeseen results. The phrases "scientific management" and "efficiency" became the stock-in-trade of numberless amateurs and pretenders, the value of the movement was magnified beyond all reason, and the public were led to believe that some wonderful new and potent instrument for getting rich quickly had been discovered.[80]

He explained that the book was a take-off from his and Alford's article and stressed that the ASME subcommittee on Administration had endorsed their three principles, even though it did tack on a fourth—the transfer of skill.[81]

Limits were immediately placed on the scope of the book. While there were two elements of an industrial undertaking, the book would center on the administrative element and not on the determinative element, "which settles the manufacturing *policy* of the business—where to sell and by what means."[82] Church deduced that there were too many unknown and variable factors present in the determinative element to derive principles at that time.[83] Another restriction of scope was imposed: Church limited his field to questions of manufacturing management.[84]

Church describe his system as "organic."

It may be desirable to explain in some detail just what is meant by the term *"organic."* The analogy of the human body gives the simplest illustration: the work of the great and lesser "organs" of the body, the heart, lungs, brain, etc., is independent yet co-ordinated. One of these organs may be working at a higher efficiency than the others, or vice versa, but on the balanced working of the whole set depends the health of the man, and his efficiency for whatever he wants to do—riding, walking, writing a poem, or dictating a business letter. Some of these organs may fall into a state of inefficiency without marked results being at once visible, or again some one of them may be permanently lowered in efficiency without hindrance to particular kinds of work. But with each there is point beyond which organic inefficiency cannot go without disaster.[85]

He then stressed the nervous system of the body, a rather frequently used analogy for him.[86] "Places where the management is always fussing over the mistakes of subordinates are places where the subordinate ganglia have failed to acquire proper habit."[87]

In a skillful fashion, Church introduced two terms, "analysis" and "synthesis."

The problem of management, broadly regarded, consists in the practical application of two great intellectual processes. Whatever the end aimed at, whether the conduct of a military campaign or the manufacture of an industrial product, the processes involved are those of analysis and synthesis. In proportion as analysis is keen and correct, and synthesis is sure and unerring, so will be the resulting efficiency. If our power of synthesis is less than our power of analysis, academic and theoretical "systems" will result. If, on the contrary, we neglect analysis and force synthesis without having shrewdly studied our ground, some and even considerable, practical success may result, but there will be a great waste of opportunity and failure to attain the most efficient results.[88]

Analysis focused on cost accounting, so that the money value of each of these very small steps can be known and compared.[89] Time study is closely allied to this comparison. The small shop analogy was then extended to jobs and to machine layout.[90] He contrasted analysis and synthesis. "Analysis is not a constructive instrument. We can make nothing by its aid. It distinguishes, it provides very accurate knowledge, it eliminates, but it does not build. That is the task of synthesis."[91] As Church explained, it is the synthesis component that makes different industries and factories different.[92]

The five organic functions were then noted: Design, Equipment, Control, Comparison, and Operation.[93] Church concluded his overview chapter with a review of synthesis and analysis.

> The art of managing an industrial plant so as to effect production most efficiently must be recognized therefore as consisting of two parts. First, the right use of synthesis—determination of the kind of organic functions needed to be set up, their due proportion, their proper balance, and their internal organization; and secondly, the right use of analysis—the investigation of the minute steps, the small stages by which product advances from stage to stage from the status of raw material to the status of finished goods. Of these two parts, the correct use of synthesis is by far the most important, as will be understood when it is realized that the systematic use of analysis is only now being introduced into industry. All the not inconsiderable triumphs of industry in the past were realized with a trifling use of analysis, and that mostly instinctive and unconscious."[94]

In a methodic pace, Church slowly built up the organic functions. "(1) Design, which *originates;* (2) Equipment, which provides physical *conditions;* (3) Control, which specifies duties, and which *orders;* (4) Comparison, which measures, records, and *compares;* and (5) Operation, which *makes.*"[95] Design precedes the other functions[96] and must be regarded as incomplete "until *all* the specifications *that it is intended to make in advance* are equally completed."[97] He limited the design function by stating "*The technical efficiency of design is not a part of the science of administration.*"[98] Operation was defined as the "*Alteration of the status of materials in accordance with previously determined design.*"[99]

Design and Operation were the two primal functions of administration; the other three—equipment, control, and comparison—were once secondary but this was no longer true in large plants.[100] Equipment had two aspects of efficiency—installation and maintenance.[101]

> Efficiency of Equipment naturally has two aspects, one of which may be called the installation, and the other the current or administrative aspect. In the installation division must be placed the selection and the arrangement of the Equipment, including the very important question of space-utilization, or lay-out, the suitability of each part of the site and buildings for the purpose to which it has been allotted, the question whether this or that method of generating and transmitting power should be adopted, the provision of proper storage bins, racks and fixtures, the mechanical means of handling material by cranes, travellers, conveyors, trucks, industrial railways and so forth, and the grouping of operative machines.[102]

Control seeks to move things.[103] Church once again used his analogy of the nervous system.

> Control, like Equipment, has its installation as well as its administrative aspect. In the former sphere it fixes the relations of persons throughout the plant. In the latter sphere it selects the right personalities to fill the posts whose duties are thus fixed, and supervises their daily performance of these duties. Control is, in fact, the nervous system (or more correctly one-half of the nervous system, the other half being Comparison) of manufacturing administration. The analogy is indeed very close. It conveys orders from the central brain (the executive), it responds to stimuli from without, and it is more than a mere telegraph system of nerves, for it has well marked ganglia, or secondary nervous centres, forming local subordinate brains concerned with special duties (stores departments, pay departments, and so forth), and responding automatically to stimuli without the central brain being concerned.[104]

Overall, control is *function which co-ordinates all the other functions* and, in addition, *supervises* their work.[105] As always though Church avoided being too abstract with such a concept by emphasizing the important human element of leadership. Church's main thrust was to design the ideal functions managers should perform. "The object of studying managerial principles is not to supersede leadership, but to discover the most efficient system of devolution of functions for the competent leader to use."[106]

Since comparison is the organ that systematically accumulates experience, "It is therefore the function *which makes use of existing standards,* and also compiles the data that enables us to revise these standards from time to time."[107] Its great instrument is measurement—the substitution of quantitative for qualitative methods wherever possible.[108] To illustrate better this concept, the nervous system analogy was again used.

> Comparison, it has already been stated above, is to be likened to the receptive half of the nervous system of the body. It has its sub-organs of sense, its clocks, time recorders, weighing machines, scales, counting machines, chemical and mechanical apparatus for testing, just as the nervous system has the five senses of sight, feeling, taste, hearing, and smell. Its office, then, is first to measure, then to record, and finally to compare. In practice, it is the counterpart of Control, since its function is to report the results of orders and instructions, and, by comparison with standards, ascertain whether these orders have successfully attained their end.[109]

Church had a very broad scope for accounting in the comparison function.

> The accounting side of Comparison is concerned with figures rather than with properties. It does not investigate, it only records, groups, and compares figures. But here, again, it looks for agreement with certain expected figures, or in other words with standards. While the great field of accounting is the record and comparison of values, still it has other fields also. Certain efficiencies are measured in time, such as the attendance of employees, the utilized and idle time of machines, periods of maturing or seasoning in certain industries; and many more are correlated with time, such as the power demand, variations of pressure or vacuum, of heat, etc. Other efficiencies are measured by number or weight, such as the conformity to standards set by the firm for maxima and minima of stores and stocks, weight of fuel consumed per quantity of water evaporated, weights of the different components of mixtures, in accordance with specifications of Design, and so forth.[110]

He then brought out the three principles of management now labeled "laws of effort" that he and Alford had already delineated. "(1) Experience must be systematically accumulated, standardized, and applied."[111] "(2) Effort must be economically regulated."[112] "(3) Personal effectiveness must be promoted."[113] Church did expand the specifics of the third principle by these sub-principles.

> 3a. Good physical conditions and environment must be maintained.
> 3b. The vocation, task, or duty should be analyzed to determine the special human faculty concerned.
> 3c. Tests should be applied to determine in what degree candidates possess special faculty.
> 3d. Habit should be formed on standardized bases, old or new.
> 3e. *Esprit de corps* must be fostered.
> 3f. Incentive must be proportioned to effort expected.[114]

The second principle was further described.

> DIVISION is the analytical principle. It decides the nature of the units to which Effort is to be applied, and thus determines the direction of Effort.
> CO-ORDINATION is the synthetical principle. It requires that all the divided units of Effort, taken together, shall amount to the result desired, exactly, i.e., without gap or overlap.
> CONSERVATION is the quantitative principle. It demands that for the given purpose the minimum amount of Effort should be used. It seeks to eliminate wasteful methods.
> REMUNERATION has to do with ascertaining, in each organic function, what is the particular feature of Effort that is to be encouraged and rewarded.[115]

Church used the installation of equipment as an example of the principle[116] and equipment was again used as an example for the co-ordination of effort sub-principle.

> Co-ordination of Effort in Equipment—In regard to Installation of Equipment. Co-ordination implies a correct balance of the different kinds. Each kind must be present in the right proportion and in the right quantity. Each Department must also be allotted the proportional amount of space fitted to its needs. These matters are generally given attention when a new plant is being started up, though even then, too little attention is frequently given to the subsidiary departments and equipment, such as storage equipment, convenient and well-planned methods of handling product, etc. But the most frequent fault in installation of the organic function of Equipment is disregard of the probable necessity for expansion. It is too frequently overlooked that an increase in business will bring in its train expansion of the subsidiary departments as well as the shops. The result of this is often disastrous.[117]

Church was also of the opinion that time study was extremely effective in establishing new and better work habits.[118] But Church cautioned that the procedure of time study should be conducted off the shop floor.[119] He wanted to limit the role of committees to advising the executive, similar to a council of war called by a general just before an important step in a campaign.[120] He was quite clairvoyant in discussing conservation of effort for the topic of machinery used in the accounting function.

> In practice, this principle of Conservation is frequently and persistently ignored. The introduction of mechanical appliances into accounting has not been an unmixed blessing, because too often the work has been fitted to the machine rather than the machine used as an aid to indispensable work. As a consequence, large and beautiful sheets of figures, full of detail, are prepared, though such detail is rarely or never consulted, and could be made available by other means if really wanted...[121]

In Church and Alford's third principle of management, which Church labeled the third law of effort in 1914, personal effectiveness must be promoted. He was both positive and realistic in his view of mankind.

> Every properly constituted young man believes that supreme attainment in almost any line of human endeavor is within his grasp. His remaining years are spent, too often, in discovering his limitations, and in undergoing the painful process of disillusionment. While ambition is the most powerful lever of success, disappointed ambition, on the other hand, is frequently a deadly blight on the energies. As industry develops, particular types of mind, habit and character find certain directions closed to them, and certain other directions more open to them than to others. A man is not just a man, he is a particular and specialized combination of powers, faculties and weaknesses, and as civilization becomes more complex, the importance of recognizing this becomes more important both to the individual and to society at large.[122]

Management would find it more difficult to deal with workers within the new field of industrial psychology. For example, Church was convinced that men would manipulate their behavior to give the appearance of doing well.[123]

It is interesting to note his differentiation between habit as far as work and the personal views held by workers.

> In speaking of habit it must be remembered here that we are not concerned with ethics, but with administration. We have nothing to do with the personal habits of men, whether they drink or smoke, whether they play cards or billiards, whether they are meat eaters or vegetarians. Still less have we to concern ourselves with their mental habits outside of industry... Nothing is more fraught with danger to industrial peace than a spirit of meddlesomeness with matters that are no real concern of the employer. He is not his employees' keeper—indeed he has a sufficiently large task if he confines his horizon to the actions of the employee in his industrial capacity.[124]

Church's insightful comment on worker incentives was valuable to managers. "The object of incentive was found to be, not an attempt to raise men of one grade to another and higher grade, for that is their personal affair, but to call out the *full use* of the faculties that may be reasonably expected to be possessed in any given grade."[125]

Although Church employed terms like "team work" and *"espirit de corps,"* he considered them too elusive to be defined in a rigorous manner.[126] Still, Church was convinced that some sort of group reward system should be developed.

> It is, then, a form of Incentive, and it can, moreover, be converted from a moral to a material incentive by the equally simple step of attaching some bonus, or small increase of pay, to the maintenance of satisfactory conditions and to the improvement of the record.
>
> It must be noted that there is a great difference both in aim and result between incentive applied in this way, and the ordinary individual piece-work or bonus system. The latter has its place, of course, and is not excluded by, nor does it exclude, the former. The one is individual; the other is, in a small way, social. Both appeal to the self-interest of men, but in a wholly different way. The one appeals to self-interest alone, the other appeals to group-pride.[127]

Bonus money should be an addition to the customary wages in the trade.[128] He seemingly was in favor of the "open the books to workers" philosophy.

> The fact is that there are but two elements to the question of the individual worker's remuneration, one of those being an absolute square deal between both sides, and the second being adequate data to enable both parties to perceive what a square deal implies. The first of those requirements is obviously a matter not of any kind of system of management or any practical device, but of personality alone; the second is mainly a matter of knowledge of facts—that is, of a method of determining prices and of accounting that commands the confidence of both sides.[129]

He also wrote about the "learning curve". "In any system of task work, *long repeated,* it is evident that increasing skill will render the original determination out of date—unless it is assumed that time-study is capable of foreseeing and allowing for such increase of skill."[130]

The organic function of design mandated a detailed "Book of the Plant." Such a record took the form of a catalogue of components or parts of jigs and tools associated with them, and of auxiliary tools such as drills, boring bars, taps, reamers, cutters, and so forth. A clear statement of the range and capacity of each machine should also be made.[131] "...A good system of classifying process should give rise to a very complete mastery over the details of the sphere of action of every machine in the plant..." "Equipment must be arranged so that product, persons and communications follow the path of least effort."[132] As one might expect, he continued his campaign against idle machinery.

> To illustrate a few of the ways in which a close scrutiny of the periods of idleness may be useful, we may consider the machine that "is not much used". It is an old friend. Physically we ignore it, as we pass by. But its reproachful presence, day after day, week after week, on our "idle-time" chart, will possibly lead to a job being schemed out suitable for it...[133]

In his 1914 book, Church finally articulated what his concept of accounting was, an explanation one wishes had appeared in an earlier work. Nevertheless, accounting played a significant part in the organic function of comparison. But since it was long in forthcoming, the following definition of accounting should be read carefully.

> It may not be evident at first sight that the basis of Comparison is for the most part accounting. This is because few people understand what modern accounting really is. Popularly it is supposed to be concerned with the verification of cash and balance sheets, but this is only one branch of the subject. Accounting in its broadest sense is the practical application of the science of quantities. It measures and records, not merely cash, but every kind of quantity that is concerned in the processes of a business. It measures and records these quantities by means of general laws which are independent of the kind of quantities in-

volved, and proves the accuracy of its measurements by recognizing that every change in a quantity is necessarily merely one of a series of changes, all of which form dependent sequences.[134]

Church also began with his 1914 book his concerns about waste and how to account for it. He made quite a strong statement that the records of waste are generally worthless unless tied into the general accounting system. He was of the opinion that man was fallible in regards to concealing waste, in that workers sought ways to hide it.[135]

Jelinek credited Church with developing ideas more fundamental and inclusive than Taylor did.[136] She felt that Church's expertise in cost accounting and in general management theory was essential.[137] "Taken together, Church's contributions substantially advanced the development of unified control systems, which made possible the efficient flow of information about operations that enable managers to control their organization."[138] She stressed the importance of Church's distinction between technical and administrative knowledge and between analysis and synthesis.[139] Her summary about Church, thus, was quite favorable.

> In summary, then, Church's contributions to management thought are more extensive than his obscurity would suggest. His viewpoint of the function of management, as inclusive and coordinative, rather than merely technical or concrete, is central to management theory down to the present. Church's contributions also include, in the same global and (in his words) synthetic fashion, the view that all non-manufacturing functions are to be evaluated on their contribution to the central production process. The ideas predate the jargon of analysis of organizational "throughput" by many years. The system of cost accounting that Church developed, consonant with this thinking, was designed to permit the appropriate evaluation of subsidiary processes. These concepts also remain in use today.[140]

Litterer's detailed review was extremely favorable to Church. Litterer considered Church's concern for the function of management to be very rare for that day.[141] "In a broad sense, Taylor and most others of this period worked in a frame of reference and direction quite different from those of Church; they were concerned with making the worker more efficient as he performed his jobs, while he was concerned with making management more efficient as a function."[142] "To Church, the science of management was a much broader concept than scientific management."[143]

> To summarize then, Church was apparently the first writer to look at the entire managerial function, to try to understand its components and operation in an attempt to make it more efficient. He sought to develop an abstract model of this function which would be usable in the analysis and evaluation of the activities of management. Yet his thinking was never far removed from the difficulties and problems with which theory in this area must always be tempered. He frequently conducted his analysis in a historical framework to understand the development of problems, or of certain factors existent in the operation of businesses. Hence, Church differs markedly from many of his contemporary authors, both in his view and concept of management and in his method of analysis.[144]

Litterer concluded with the hope "that Church's work and contributions may be rescued from their current neglect."[145]

Wren placed Church in a category with Henri Fayol, because both were concerned with the functional approach to the study of management.[146] But, interestingly, Wren did not detect a universal quality to Church's writing. "The organic functions of Church do not have the logical appeal of Fayol's nor do they appear as universal in design due to Church's predilection toward manufacturing concerns."[147]

As already noted in Chapter 2, the critic Colley, who reviewed the 1914 book for *The Journal of Accountancy*, had a great knowledge of Church's background and, most likely, Church himself.[148] He joined Church in attacking the imitators of Taylor and Emerson. "In the enthusiasm of the patent medicine consumer, the manufacturer's rush to apply the nostrum of amateur's disconnected ideas has caused him to overlook the necessity of constructing the conditions insuring successful application."[149] "In these days of machine-made rules and systems advo-

68

cated and expounded by hungry amateurs, it is refreshing to find a man with Mr. Church's knowledge and experience seeking his final reliance for efficiency in the influence of a strong personality."[150] Colley concluded that "The book is a pronounced step forward along the trail blazed by Taylor and Emerson, and the work is one which will be widely read and approved."[151]

Ralph Currier Davis used numerous quotes from Church as footnote justification for his own book, *The Fundamentals of Top Management*.[152] Those justifications included Church's theories on: design,[153] planning,[154] organic,[155] devolution,[156] coordination,[157] and comparison.[158] Davis was of the opinion that "Church greatly influenced the thinking of later students of management."[159] One could easily place Davis himself in that category. As already noted in the second chapter, Church was a consultant to the Winchester Repeating Arms Company during World War I. Davis was employed there at that time. He felt that the then president of Winchester Repeating Arms Company, John E. Otterson, was heavily influenced by the writings of Emerson and Church. Otterson's philosophy attracted much attention during World War I but was unsuccessful, because of his failure to coordinate the control function.[160]

The writer of this monograph found that ideas continued to spew forth from Church. Some were new; some were related to his previous writings. There were three general sets of ideas in the 1914 book. The first set dealt with management principles and with accounting relationships to management. [Idea 57] Management is concerned with "analysis" and "synthesis"—the constructive instrument that builds. [Idea 58] "Analysis" focuses on cost accounting, which records and compares the money value of each of the very small steps in the production process. [Idea 59] "Synthesis" is the choice, the relative effectiveness, the right proportion, the right kind of means that is in question. [Idea 60] The five organic functions of management are design, equipment, control, comparison, and operation. [Idea 61] Control fixes the relations of persons throughout the plant and selects the right personalities to fill the posts. [Idea 62] The goal of comparison is to substitute quantitative for qualitative measurement methods. [Idea 63] Accounting must be concerned with efficiencies measured in time, numbers, and weight, as well as in dollars. [Idea 64] Accounting should not be governed by mechanical appliances, in that the work has been fitted to the machine rather than the machine used as an aid to indispensable work. [Idea 65] Results of operations must be controlled and safeguarded by a thoroughly modern accounting system. [Idea 66] Records of waste must be tied into the general accounting system.

The second set of ideas dealt with the worker. [Idea 67] A job should be analyzed to determine the special human faculty concerned. [Idea 68] Tests should be used to determine the faculties of the job applicants. [Idea 69] *Espirit de corps* must be fostered. [Idea 70] The technique of time study should best be conducted off the shop floor and be the basis for establishing new and better work habits. [Idea 71] Men will manipulate their behavior to give the appearance of doing well. [Idea 72] Incentive systems should call out the full use of the talents of that particular grade of worker. [Idea 73] The group bonus system can enchance group pride. [Idea 74] Workers need to have confidence in the records of the firm in the computation of the group bonus. [Idea 75] Time study must take into account the gains in skill in doing a long repeated job.

The third set of ideas dealt with machinery. [Idea 76] Each kind of equipment must be present with right proportion and in the right quantity. [Idea 77] Each department must be allocated the proportional amount of space fitted to its needs. [Idea 78] Expansion to meet new business must be planned. [Idea 79] There should be a Book of the Plant. [Idea 80] Equipment must be arranged so that product, persons, and communications follow the path of least effort. [Idea 81] There should be an idle-time chart for machinery.

In addition to harping upon familiar ideas, Church continued to use the strawman approach. However, he seemed to let up a bit on Taylor and Emerson and concentrate on warnings about their imitators. This was not only a very good strategy but very consistent with his emphasis on unique solutions worked out from his and Alford's general principles of management. He also continued the emphasis on manufacturing and, but, only on the administrative side of manufacturing. This policy decision was quite wise, as it left him in his area of strength and recognized expertise at that time. It was not until his 1923 book, *The Making of an Executive*, that he became more inclusive in his writing about distribution cost control, marketing, selling, technology, and the determinative element.

Analogies were again quite well employed. The organs of the body and the nervous system analogies are examples of those. Church showed a mastery with words with the "analysis" and "synthesis" intellectual processes. These two processes were tied into the five organic functions and his and Alford's three general principles of management. He presented a very complete package for managers. Perhaps this was his greatest achievement as a writer in the field of management. All the parts of manufacturing management were analyzed but, along with that, synthesis was achieved by the use of the three general principles of management. This writer remains puzzled by Church's switch to the three laws of effort from the previous three principles of management. This switch made it much more difficult to follow the text, as one was already quite accustomed to the three principles approach.

It is not surprising that Church focused on machinery for much of his specific discussions to illustrate the principles and functions of management. One recalls his comments on machinery at the 1912 ASME meeting. He seemingly was not as concerned about the capital procurement decision, which he probably classified as a determinative decision for management. However, once the machine was on board, he certainly had a very good grasp on it, perhaps a better grasp on it than any other writer in both accounting and management.

Out of all his writings, this work best articulated Church's views on accounting in a broad managerial setting. He was quite inclusive, much more than just dollars to be recorded in journals, ledgers, and statements. The accounting scholar DR Scott comes to mind here, as one who held and wrote similar views. Scott better developed the role that business statistics should play in accounting than Church did. But still one who is interested in getting an overall perspective of Church's accounting writings should not overlook the 1914 book.

Although Church was cognizant of the machine's influence on the work place, he never forgot the worker. Church surely was one to allow a worker the choice of his life style and his desires for advancement on the job with the limit of not placing a square peg in a round hole. It is interesting to note his attempt to develop the group bonus system as a part of *espirit de corps* and to keep time study away from the factory floor as much as possible. He was an humane man. Urwick's description of him takes on a greater meaning.

> "...Yet those few who knew him say he was an unusually charming man, one with whom it was a pleasure to work; that he had gifts, not shared by all the early "efficiency experts," for drawing out useful contributions from those with whom he worked and for finding compromise solutions which won general satisfaction.[161]

1915

Church presented a major paper at the 1915 International Engineering Congress in San Francisco during the Pan-Pacific Exhibition of that year.[162] He followed that with a series of articles in the *American Machinist* on factory reports and records.[163] These articles were revised for his 1917 book, *Manufacturing Costs and Accounts*, and were Part III of that work.[164] Since these articles were not listed in *The Engineering Index*, as the *American Machinist* was not included in that Index from 1913 through 1916,[165] nor listed in *The Accountant's Index*,[166] they were chosen for review in this section, rather than in Chapter 3 with the 1917 book.

A 26 page paper, "Industrial Management," was given at *The International Engineering Congress* in 1915.[167] It was basically a condensation of his 1914 book. Interestingly, the last paragraph offered a less enthusiastic view on the science of management than was Church's trademark during this period, even though the paragraph was consistent with his view of the importance of leadership.

> The present condition of the science or art of management is one of assimilation and digestion rather than of active change. After a period of discovery and invention has come a period of application and modification. This is likely to continue for some time. The high tide of excitement and enthusiasm caused by the introduction of analytical methods has receded, and a more dispassionate view of the situation is being taken generally. It is beginning to be realized that, just as a study of military science does not produce great generals, so a knowledge of the science of management, inasfar as it can be called a science at the present stage of its development, will not produce great managers. The man has to bring something to the study in each case.[168]

The groundwork for the four article series in 1915 was laid in the first article, "What is a Cost System?."[169] It was, in this reviewer's opinion, the best article of the series, because it was the most general. The remaining three articles tended towards the specifics, and, as such, got mired down in giving detailed examples. These examples may have led Church into the same trap he had warned others about—the trap of blind imitation. But, unlike the other three, the first article focused on reporting information for four different managers—shop foremen, superintendent, executive, and proprietor.[170] He used an analogy of an expensive machine whose use was not fully understood to a cost system from which few people really know what they have the right to expect.[171] And, of course, the article wasn't complete without one more dig at what Church now labeled "commercial accountants."

> Another cause of trouble is that the design of a cost system may be approached from two opposite viewpoints—that of the commercial accountant, who thinks in ledger accounts, and that of the shop staff, who think in terms of hours, men and materials. The accountant thinks of detail as a troublesome necessity; the shop staff know that detail is the life-blood of a cost system provided it is available at the right time and in the right place.[172]

Church wrote that the foreman wants to have brought to his attention a process or operation which is exceptional.[173] Church had quite demanding goals for the basic records which "...should indicate the man, the machine, the nature of the process (if more than one process can be affected by the machine), the job number, and a complete record of the starts and stops, the interruptions, the overtime belonging to the job. Any time record worth its salt should provide all these details in readable form."[174] Immediate recording is needed for immediate discussion of the documents with the delinquent.[175] The foreman is also to be concerned with machine idle time,[176] orders on hand,[177] and spoiled work.[178]

> The daily returns of exceptional jobs and spoiled work will contain items that go against sundry workmen. A record should therefore be kept for each man, to include reference to all such losses, and also his bonus earnings, late attendance, and other data against him or in his favor. With properly designed methods such a record can be compiled at little expense, and will be first-hand evidence of each man's value.[179]

The foreman is interested in details, then, whereas the superintendent is more interested in broad results. Rather than being interested in each process, the superintendent is interested in the overall timing and cost of an order. "The superintendent control of orders should be based on a 'master schedule' listing all the different components belonging to an order, and against each component, all the different processes to be carried out on it."[180] He needs more detailed information on indirect expenses than does the foreman.[181] He is interested in three types of departmental efficiency—(1) men; (2) machines; and (3) wastes.[182]

The executive, on the other hand, is to be provided with monthly results and has a comparatively smaller interest in cost accounts. He is most concerned about the monthly budget/actual reports. The proprietor focuses on the monthly net income and the end of the month balance sheet. To demonstrate the inter-relationships of all four reporting parties, Church used the pyramid example of reports, in which "each stage should be built up in more and more general terms from detail that was verified at the beginning."[183]

The second article, "What a Foreman Should Know About Costs", gave illustrations of various control forms, like a time card.[184] Church then described a shop album, which was books of blank sheets, one for each order and containing as many as there were components in the order.[185] There was to be a posting of information for each time card.[186] The quickest way of doing this was by dissecting the time cards and sorting the sections according to their order numbers. This was to be done rapidly by a paper cutter with a suitable guard. The time cards were sliced up into sections, and then sections were sorted in properly designed trays, first to thousands, then to hundreds and later to tens and units.[187] For as Church explained, "Detail must be piping-hot or it is of slender value. The people who make the detail are the people who can use the detail."[188]

The next article in the series, "What the Superintendent Should Know,"[189] conveyed a master schedule which controlled all the sequences of work done. "Inspection of the schedule at any moment will show the condition of the order as regards completion, the degree of delay already incurred, the extent to which the cost is coming out as expected with references to standard, and the cost to date of all finished parts on the order."[190] Church then went on to illustrate and describe the following forms: finished-order stub, finished-order list, spoiled-work register, list of machine earnings, unfinished jobs in shops, burden schedule, wages report, stores report, factory burden, production report, unabsorbed burden report, additions to equipment report, equipment report, sales burden report, and collectible accounts report.[191] As this writer mentioned earlier, such a list of particulars may tend to be interpreted as being a list to imitate, rather than a sample of a solution applied to one company.

The last article of the series was "What the Executive Wants to Know About Costs."[192] Church was of the opinion that "The ordinary profit and loss account and balance sheet are derived from mercantile practice, and are much older than modern manufacturing. For this reason, they do not commonly present the facts in a strictly logical order..."[193] He went on to illustrate and describe the following forms: wages report, stores report, administration-expense distribution, factory burden report, production report, additions to equipment report, equipment report, sales-burden report, trading report, and collectible-accounts report.[194] He very much favored a budget/actual comparison for businesses of an established character.[195]

Church's approach was immediately attacked in the Discussion of Previous Questions section of the American Machinist by C.J. Morrison,[196] who argued for a cost clerk, rather than a productive worker, to do the work that Church recommended.

> ...The method of making a time record has frequently been observed to be about as follows: Stop work, clean hands, get time card, hunt for pencil, borrow pencil, consult clock, make entry on card, break point of pencil, hunt for knife, borrow knife, sharpen pencil, consult clock, make entries on card, put away card, return pencil, return knife, resume work.[197]

Jenckes in the same section two weeks later also was concerned about the big increase in labor due to Church's system. Jenckes described his system in detail and posed this question to Church. "Can the shop album be incorporated in my system without causing more labor than its advantage warrant?"[198]

The writer of this monograph found that the ideas from this section deal with reports and their timing. [Idea 82] The foreman must have exceptional matters brought to his attention. [Idea 83] Immediate recording is needed for immediate discussions to be held. Detail must be piping-hot. The people who make the detail are the people who can use the detail. [Idea 84] There should be a master schedule which controls all the sequences of work done. [Idea 85] Budget/actual comparisons should be made.

On a more subjective note, the 1915 articles showed Church at his very best, when he delineated the theory of the four levels of reporting, and at his not so very best, when he overwhelmed the reader with a myriad of reports. These articles must have been extremely confusing to those readers not very familiar with his past writings, as many of the reports

72

were based on the machine-hour rate method. In the lexicon of today, Church would have been accused of "information overload." Be that as it may, these articles represent an important part of the totality of Church's writings and provide a very important link between his management and accounting efforts. These articles do tie-in how control was to be reported from the lowest level of the organization to the highest. It is extremely unfortunate that they were not included in either *The Accountants Index: 1920* nor the *Engineering Index*. Anyone interested in a worthwhile long-term project might consider updating these two important reference books.

1923

Church, who listed himself as an Industrial Economist on the title page, expanded his comments on the management of the firm to include other areas than manufacturing in his 1923 book, *The Making of an Executive*. A more popular-press type book, it was tailored, as the title implied, for the executive. Yet, the text was choppy because the numbered paragraphs tended to be tight summaries of very broad areas. It was originally published by D. Appleton and Company in 1923 but also issued in 1922 as a 10 part series in three volumes by the International Textbook Company, by Winston in its Business Library for Businessmen series, and by the International Library of Technology in 1926.[199] This review concentrates on the newer areas of coverage by Church in the 1923 Appleton book.

This book was written for the executive. "The aim of the book is to give the reader in condensed form a connected idea of the fundamentals of business organization and routine, which knowledge every executive must possess."[200] The book not only covered routines and layouts but also covered the human side of business as well.[201] Church was ready to admit that "Business administration has practically developed into a definite profession."[202] The work of the executive is general in nature and he creates his own scope of work, as opportunity is always knocking at his door.[203] Church wanted the executive to be imbued with the modern spirit of broadened understanding, as a result of contacts with the ideas and methods that had become standardized in the profession.[204] His definition of the scientific method is worth noting.

> In general the scientific method depends on taking nothing for granted, and becoming familiar not only with broad or practical results, but also with the infinitely small influences and conditions that go to build up results of all kinds, both successful and unsuccessful. In other words, it is mastery of minute details and of fundamental principles that is aimed at.[205]

His concern about "wastes" was presented in a broader fashion than it had received in his other writings. Even a correction of a small error could lead to accumulated savings of an important amount. He stressed the importance of utilizing commercial wastes and by-products with better marketing of them.[206] The executive was to beware of his competitors and continually be on the search for new ideas, new machinery, and new methods. As one might expect, "habit" played an important role in the qualities of the executive. The defects of mental untidiness and inexactness can be corrected to some degree.[207] But a tendency toward vagueness can be a manager's downfall. "Vagueness of all kinds is one of the great business pitfalls."[208]

Church wanted the executive to be quite knowledgeable of financing, because it "...is more potent for good and evil than any of the other departments, since, in a sense, it is the regulator of them all."[209] The executive also must know about meters and recorders, as modern business is being increasingly based on measurement, as well as about calculating and statistical machines.[210] "...Just as an artist must first learn the use of his brushes and colors before he can begin to paint, so the would-be executive must understand the range and application of these new instruments if he would find the key to success."[211]

The executive also must have control over both investment in material but also the amount of future liability being incurred by the purchasing department. Graphs should be used in both cases.[212]

He was much more expansive on the coverage of the marketing role.

—When product has been manufactured it has to be marketed. or sold. Marketing is a very different kind of activity from those already considered. but in the main, the same principles of layout, routing, and graphic representation are applied in the organization of this branch of business. This organization will cover the following points: (a) Consideration of the product and its adaptability to the market; this study should include not only the actual product itself, but also the methods of packing, casing, labeling, and so forth, that facilitate handling at various stages. (b) Careful study of the field or area in which the product is to be offered. Modern methods of analyzing the capacity of the field to absorb the product are highly developed. and include classification of prospective customers, layout of sales area, routing of traveling men, location of branch offices or distribution points, etc. (c) Organization of a sales department. (d) Development of methods by which the executive is posted on the general trend of the marketing operations.[213]

The executive should be in full touch with the marketing function, as that was the only function which brought money into the business.[214] For as Church said, once a customer is on the books, he should be a permanent asset to the business.[215] Such statistics as selling costs per inquiry and per order should be collected, as well as business volume by sales fields and by customers.[216]

The coverage about the technical side of business was also expanded. No longer did he just assume this side was well run.

Technical betterment has to do with trade knowledge. Almost every business has a technical side as well as a management and commercial side. Engineering, mechanical, and chemical data must be systematically collected and indexed for the use of the technical and operative staffs. Progress in such matters is always going on. Patents are being taken out, papers are being read before technical societies, information is published in trade papers, all of which cannot be ignored, but should on the contrary be kept prominently before the attention of such persons as are concerned with technical processes. Such information should also be disseminated amongst workers to encourage them to take an interest in their work and fit themselves for better positions.[217]

Graphic presentations in various formats were covered in the book,[218] as was the analysis topic.[219] The principles of layout were discussed[220] and then visual controls[221] and mechanical aids.[222] One of Church's most remarkable passages, though, is on counting devices.

Counting appliances are very numerous, both in type and in the uses to which they are put. In general they are used as a check on operation. As a rule their action depends on counting the revolutions of some axle or shaft, but sometimes actual working strokes are counted instead of machine motion. Such counters are of three main types—dial counters, of which the speedometer used on automobiles is the best known example; graphic recording counters, in which the record is traced on a card or ribbon. detached at intervals for study; and electrically connected counters, in which the record is made at a distance (say in the office of the superintendent) from the machine whose record is being taken. There is no doubt that, in most industries in which operation is more or less intermittent, it will pay to attach a recorder to every operative machine, and to make the records a matter of careful tabulation and charting.[223]

Metering, therefore, was quite important to stop guesswork.[224] A forerunner of the data processing card was shown and the management by exception principle was once again stressed.[225]

He devoted 54 pages to the chapter, "The Executive and the Office."[226] He stressed that the subject of office organization has not as yet received anything like the attention that has been given to the problem of organization in the productive departments.[227] Church was very concerned about the manifold copies of an order system,[228] not to mention the unit cost of office operations.[229] Moreover, Church strongly suggested the implementation of a specific department to deal solely with handling customer complaints.

A separate division for dealing with complaints will be necessary only in businesses in which a very large number of small transactions with customers take place, as, for example, in a mail order business. But in all cases, even though a separately organized division is not advisable, the responsibility for attention to complaints should be allotted quite definitely to some one official. Every letter that contains a complaint of any kind should be brought to his attention by the readers who open the mail.[230]

"Purchasing and Storekeeping" occupied the next 55 pages.[231] The main point here was that a technical department should be involved with material specifications.[232] In addition, Church did a very nice job explaining the contradictions of the three factors of purchasing.

> ...To attain success an agent must continually wrestle with three mutually opposing factors, and his success will depend on the manner in which he reconciles these oppositions. From the viewpoint of the general executive that purchasing department is most successfully run which:
>
> 1. Maintains the current stocks of material as low as possible.
> 2. Does its buying on the most favorable terms.
> 3. Keeps the productive departments supplied, with the minimum of delay.
>
> It will be noticed that these three factors of successful purchasing are, in a measure, mutually opposed...[233]

He stressed the importance of a chart which offered visual control of purchase orders, so that not only the purchasing department but also other interested departments could utilize a purchase order control board.[234]

He wrote 50 pages on "The Executive and the Factory,"[235] a topic well-covered in his other writings both in management and accounting. Still, a section on specialized machines was unique to the work.

> ...Hand operative skill can be changed rapidly, by the simple process of firing and hiring, but not so machines. They represent locked-up capital, and, if they cannot be kept at work, represent a dead loss. As a general principle, specialized machines should not be installed unless there is practical assurance that they can be kept working to their full capacity. This implies a continuous flow of business of precisely the kind that the machine will do. If there is doubt of this, then it will be better in most instances to set up a general machine to do the work, even though it may be less economical. The whole business, however, goes far back to the original question of design. The prospective manufacturer must know clearly what he is about. Then, having settled exactly what line of work is to be taken up, let him abide by that. Let him not seek or accept business for which the plant is not perfectly fitted.[236]

Church repeated his philosophy of keeping machines at work with an emphasis now on how idle machines affected individuals at a plant, including the executive. "An idle machine is a constant reproach to the foreman, to the planning department, to the sales department, and, not least, to the executive. To which of these it is the worst reproach depends on why it is idle..."[237] He seemed to have modified his position on the supplementary rate by 1923, even though it was only in 1930 he did so in an accounting book.

> ...But this increased cost cannot be recovered from the customer. It is therefore of no service for estimating or bidding on new business. By the device of the hourly rate, however, the order costs, officially, that is, on the books, no more in slack than in busy times, other things being equal. But the unabsorbed burden is much greater. This unabsorbed burden, however it is regarded, must be charged to profit and loss account. There is no one who can be made to pay for it. It is therefore better to keep this unabsorbed burden entirely separate from true cost. This is just what is done by establishing for the use of machines an hourly rate independent of the state of trade. The method must be used with caution, but when so used has important advantages.[238]

Chapter VI, "Marketing the Product," contained 49 pages of material never tackled by Church as a package.[239] He felt that while the crystallization of selling principles was not yet in sight, there still were many reasons for every executive to study the field.[240] He was concerned with the appearance of the product, even machinery.[241] He was also very concerned about the executive's underestimation of the marketing function.

The possession of a good product does not mean the possession of a good profit. Mechanically or technically a thing may be excellent, but its commercial value may be very little. It may be useful as a side line and no more. Many little specialty plants are founded, only to disappear in a short time, just because the expense of selling the article takes all the profits. The cost of a thing made is a very different matter from the cost of the same thing sold. The world is full of wonderful devices and appliances that lack supporters. Why? Because, though it is easy to set up a plant and make these things, it would require much capital to keep the field until the ideas embodied in the devices were sold to the ultimate consumer. It is not surprising, therefore, that the modern sales promoter begins by ascertaining what relation his product has to the possible users or consumers.[242]

Church was quite cautious about advertising expenditures, which only could lay a favorable seed bed.[243] He also limited the role of a "natural salesman" to specialty firms and favored a standardized approach and training for the "average salesman."[244] A sales manual was crucial.

...Frequently it will be found desirable to include a brief and condensed course of salesmanship, showing how to approach the customer and to arouse his interest; when not to press him; when to close the order; and setting forth the rules and regulations of the firm as regards the routine reports, expense accounts, etc., of the individual salesman. Manuals of this kind will hardly convert a poor salesman into a good one, but they will give all, good and poor alike, the best possible groundwork on which to erect a good record. It will be readily understood that a great deal will depend on the manner in which the manual itself is prepared.[245]

The salesman's route should be laid out for him and quotas should be assigned.[246]

Church demanded a very descriptive system for recording sales—date, customer's reference number, salesman's number, class of goods, stock number, size, number of items sold, weight sold, gross sales price, net sales price, cost price, and credit allowed in days.[247] Unit costs of inquiries are important and should be portrayed graphically.[248] There should be customer graphs by location. "Any persistent drooping or sudden stop in a customer's curve will point the need for inquiry."[249]

Chapter VII, "Employment, Welfare, and Labor" covered 38 pages.[250] While Church, on one hand, held a commodity view of labor,[251] he countered that view with a broad, humanitarian viewpoint.

...If the executive takes a broadminded view of the matter, realizing that employees are human beings and that it pays, in the strictest business sense, to study, and even to some extent to humor, their peculiarities, a very different atmosphere will be created in the plant, than if he looks on the wage-earner as an untrustworthy tool, to be sharpened by continual friction, and thrownout at the slightest signs of inefficiency...[252]

He warned against the notion of "industrial democracy", unless each worker brought something to the common stock.[253] However, the executive must "...know as exactly as possible, the inclusive and general conditions under which the human creature functions best as a worker."[254] He seemed to anticipate the "Hawthorne Study" with this comment.

The phrase physical comfort requires no explanation. Everyone understands that for physical comfort a man requires such things as a suitable temperature, so that he shall be neither too hot nor too cold; he must have time to eat and drink; plenty of light for working; sweet, pure air, free from fumes, to breathe; and so on. A little less obvious, perhaps, is the phrase psychological environment. And yet, it is clear enough. Everyone knows that true comfort depends, not only on such physical conditions as those enumerated, but also on a man's state of mind, and on the conditions, the psychological environment, that determine this state of mind. He must feel at home in his surroundings, not oppressed by fear of those over him, nor by fear of dangers that may lie in his path; he must not live in a maze by reason of imperfectly understood instructions, nor be hampered by rules and regulations impossible to observe; but on the contrary, he must understand his job, have confidence in his superiors, feel at home among his mates, be free from care through exposure to unnecessary dangers, and must generally pass a contented and happy day, with reasonable joy in his work, and a feeling that life is not a miserable round of petty annoyances and petty tyrannies. Under such conditions, it is probable that his work will be more satisfactory, both to himself and to his employer, in quality and quantity. The modern idea is to develop just such arrangements in the internal organization as will induce this condition of psychological contentment, simply because it is found, as a matter of stern practice, that it pays to do so.[255]

Church wanted the same care extended to purchasing labor as to the purchase of material.[256] A card system should be established for each worker, in which information would be gathered on Physical Strength, Good English, Apprehension, Forcefulness, Patience, Personality, Manual Dexterity, Special Skill Claimed, and Has Worked As.[257] In addition to keeping track of an employee, Church favored decisions made by an employee committee to paternalistic decisions.

Better than the method of making unsolicited gifts, which always smacks of paternalism, is a plan giving the workers opportunity to air their own views, and to formulate plans for the approval of the executive. This has a two-fold influence. First, it really does insure that improvements actually desired shall receive first consideration; and second, it cultivates a sense of responsibility in the worker, and transfers the target of criticism of the habitual grumbler from the management to his fellow-workers, who are usually capable of taking care of themselves. The customary procedure is to set up committees, each covering some fundamental point, such as safety, sanitation, fire protection, etc....[258]

The committee idea, therefore, was based on the philosophy that the worker was an individual with outside interests, not just an automated body performing a specific job. "...The committee idea is really based on this fact. Because a man is a mechanic or a draftsman of some kind it does not follow that he is only a mechanic or a craftsman. He may be a musician, or an orator, or an amateur photographer of skill. Or he may have a head for business detail..."[259]

Chapter VIII, "Promotion of Quality and Quantity," had 39 pages[260] of information covered in Church's previous writings. Church did expand his discussion of the limitations of the group bonus in the light of plant accounting.

The group bonus system cannot very well be applied indiscriminately to all kinds of industry... Where the product of a shop is very varied in character, as, for example, in some machine shops, the chances of introducing the method with effect are not so good. The group bonus is particularly adapted to those cases in which the workers are unable to control the speed of operation but may do much by subsidiary activities to effect savings that would be difficult to secure in any other way. The method does not preclude the application of piecework at the same time; but it is chiefly applicable in work that does not lend itself to a basis of individual contracts with the workers.[261]

Chapter IX, "The Executive and Finance," had 46 pages [262] and was a little more informative of his views on accounting and accountants than his other writings. Unfortunately, some of the views were muddled. For instance, his view of the end aim of all accounting as "to set up a comparison between ownership on the one hand and on the other hand property, technically called assets, after allowing for all debts owing to the company" is quite limited in scope.[263] He tried to differentiate between "profit" and "surplus." "Surplus is profit only when it is in a form withdrawable from the business as cash, and distributable as dividend."[264] An accounting instructor would expect a better sentence from a first year accounting student than that. Church muddled the "Depreciation Reserve" account with the "reserve fund" concept of depreciation.[265] He seemed to adopt an entity theory of accounting.

Something must now be said about the right-hand side of the balance sheet. Hitherto this has been considered in its principal function of exhibiting the distribution of Ownership. In practice this side of the sheet is commonly called, not the Ownership, but the Liability side. This requires explanation. The matter is simple if the right viewpoint is adopted.

The balance sheet is a list of property, primarily. It is an inventory of a business, of a particular business. But more especially it is a statement by the management of the business, not by the owner. Consequently, it has to show on the one side the inventory of assets: on the other, just to whom the management is liable, or to whom it is responsible, for the care of these assets. This liability of the management may be to a single owner, or to many owners, but it is always a liability.[266]

He did better when discussing the Balance Sheet and current valuation which he felt should be left to the executive and not to the accountant or the auditor.[267] Once Church left "commercial accounting", he was back home in cost accounting. He replaced the term "production factors" by "service departments."[268] He was more explicit about the budgeting area.

...The principle of budgeting is a simple one. It consists primarily in listing all items of expenditure in advance of their maturity. But this alone would not be of much service, because items might well be forgotten even then. Budgeting is nothing less than the systematic forecasting of the financial status of all divisions of the business. For this purpose, each department is gone over with a fine tooth comb, and all possible avenues of expenditure are listed. The previous year's accounts are called on to provide information. In the case of a new business, an experienced cost accountant should be relied on to make up the first budget, which should, moreover, be submitted to the scrutiny of all heads of departments, so that no item shall be omitted. It will readily be understood that an imperfect budget, that is, one in which important items were not represented, would be worse than no budget at all, for the reason that it might beget an unjustifiable confidence.[269]

Expected and actual figures were to be utilized.[270] The sales budget must be made in great detail, since the sales forecast has an important bearing on the expenditures budget.[271]

The last chapter "Reconstruction, Betterment, and Planning" was quite new for Church, because it included topics of a "deterministic" nature that had been assumed away in the past. The chapter contained 36 pages.[272] There was a scientific aspect, if not a scientific basis, to all industry.[273] The first step to manage this scientific aspect was to establish a research organization to collect systematically all information on the materials and processes of the product.

The technical and trade magazines will form another quarry that must be carefully and systematically worked. The search should not be confined to home sources, but should include foreign publications, notably those in England, France, and Germany. When necessary, translations should be made of important papers. All this involves some expense, but in a plant of any considerable size such expense fully justifies itself. A few ideas, even minor ones, discovered and applied each year, will amply repay the cost. Moreover, the satisfaction of knowing that nothing involving the improvement of the product or the welfare of the industry can happen without being noticed should be a matter of satisfaction to the progressive executive.[274]

He recommended a technical library, headed by an elderly or a former operating executive sidelined because of an illness. Such a library would help establish a good communication network to convey important matters.[275] Church gave the standard classification of research in its pure and its applied aspects. Again, he was concerned about wastes.

...As for the opportunities that present themselves in the recovery of wastes, these are well illustrated by the remark of the present owner of an old-established soap plant: "My father and my grandfather must have run into the sewers a value equal to the whole capitalization of the plant." The strong position that Germany had built up for itself in the dye industry, before the war, was earned very largely as the reward of an unremitting and extensive research campaign continued through half a century.[276]

An excellent chart was given for manufacturing betterments in which there were six major classifications: (1) Betterment in Material—(a) More Exact Specifications, (b) Reducing Wastes, and (c) Investigating New Kinds; (2) More Efficient Processes—(a) Making Time Studies, (b) Illuminating Lost Motion, and (c) Experiment on New Methods; (3) Improved Operative

Machines—(a) Improving Present Machine, (b) Increasing Power Economy, (c) Investigating New Types, and (d) Developing Auxiliary Appliances; (4) Economy in Handling Material—(a) Charting Material Improvements, (b) Rearranging Layouts, and (c) Investigating New Ways; (5) Better Working Environment—(a) Improving Physical Surroundings, (b) Safety First Propaganda, (c) Lunch Rooms, Housing, etc., and (d) Promoting Clubs and Games; and (6) Improved Labor Relations—(a) Enlisting Employee Cooperation, (b) Training of New Employees, (c) Bonus for Quality and Quantity, and (d) Introducing Committee System.[277]

The writer of this monograph found that the ideas of Church were applied to a much wider scope within a manufacturing business. He clearly must have been much more involved with the marketing function during the years between 1913 and 1923, because he surely adopted a marketing perspective and a "deterministic" perspective in his 1923 book. [Idea 86] Commercial wastes and by-products must be better marketed. [Idea 87] To insure competitiveness, the executive must continually be on the search for new ideas, new machinery, and new methods. [Idea 88] Selling costs and office costs are to be analyzed in many different ways, including unit costs. [Idea 89] A customer on the books should be a permanent asset to the business. [Idea 90] Every complaint must be analyzed by one official or one department. [Idea 91] Specialized machines should not be installed unless there is practical assurance that they can be kept working to their full capacity. [Idea 92] The executive should seek or accept business for which the plant is perfectly fitted. [Idea 93] The product, even machinery, should have a good appearance. [Idea 94] The cost of a thing made is different from the cost of the same thing sold. [Idea 95] The selling function must be routinized by use of a sales manual and by a careful layout of sales routes. [Idea 96] The sales forecast is crucial. [Idea 97] A technical library and information system must be established.

The second set of ideas dealt with financial matters. [Idea 98] Vagueness of all kinds is one of the great business pitfalls. [Idea 99] Meters and recorders, as well as calculating and statistical machines, must be known by the executive. [Idea 100] The amount of liability for outstanding purchase orders must be known by the executive. [Idea 101] The executive must balance the three factors of successful purchasing. [Idea 102] There should be a purchase-order control board. The third set of ideas were worker-oriented. [Idea 103] A card system should be established for each worker. [Idea 104] Employee committees lead to better decisions for employee social expenditures than paternalism.

It is unfortunate that this work was not as rigorously reviewed as Church's accounting works and his 1911, 1912, and 1914 writings in management. One can understand why, since it is easy to dismiss the 1923 effort as just another one of a seemingly countless series of executive how-to books of that era. Most likely one viewing the 1923 book without familiarity with his prior efforts would miss the significance of this book. However, for one who had followed him through the years, the 1923 effort is a milestone. Not only did he further elaborate on the positioning of his prior topics into an holistic treatment but he added some new topics as well. The 1923 book probably marked the high-water mark for Church as a managerial writer and, as such, must be studied by anyone wanting to get a full view of him.

Furthermore, this book reveals personal traits of Church, which upon reflection, he deemed useful to share with executives. Specifically, Urwick commented that Church had a reputation for vanishing for weeks at a time and then reappearing with a new and constructive idea.[278] This ties in with his recommending that the executive take a detached view away from the detail of the day. Undoubtedly, it was from the place—wherever it was—that this detached view took place that deterministic decisions should be made.

If there were an area in which Church could have done more in management accounting in an holistic sense, it would have been in the area of accounting and managing for "wastes." This topic came along too far after his earlier accounting writings for the type of skillful writing that would have placed the topic in the same boat as the machine hour rate method, production centers, and factors of production. But a volume on Church's discussion on wastes would be a worthwhile endeavor for any scholar interested in the topic.

He was quite clairvoyant on the topic of accounting machines, although one should not be surprised with that, in light of his interest in machinery. This was also true with his stress of counters and meters. One could wonder what great success he would have had today with the advanced measurement tools available now. Litterer's comment on the need to resurrect Church's efforts is very poignant in the measurement issue and with his use of charts, graphs, and other visual aid techniques.

Garner briefly mentioned Church's efforts in distribution costing. The early ideas of A. Hamilton Church along this line bore fruit in such treatises as *Cost Accounting for Sales* (Hilgert, 1926), *Overhead Costs in Theory and Practice* (Maken, 1933), *and Control of Distribution Cost and Sales* (Castenholz, 1930).[279] It is probable that if Church were to be credited for this topic of controlling distribution costs, his 1923 book is the place where the credit belongs.

Once again, this writer returns to his criticism of Church's apparent lack of empathy for "commercial accountants" and his apparent lack of knowledge of "commercial accounting." It is difficult for the writer to believe that Church could have been so casual in the discussions of the Balance Sheet, Surplus and Profits, and Depreciation Reserves. This casualness remains Church's Achilles heel.

CHAPTER SIX
THE FIELDS OF BUSINESS AND SOCIETY
AND OF INDUSTRIAL ENGINEERING

Church wrote in two other areas far removed from each other. The first, business and society, was quite global: the second, industrial engineering, was quite specific. The writings in both these areas are worth reviewing as they give other perspectives of Church.

Business and Society
1901 and 1917

He published two works which more pertain to the business and society general field than to the more specific field of management. In 1901 he wrote "British Industrial Welfare" and in 1917 "The Future of Industry." These articles presented his views on a more global level.

"British Industrial Welfare: The Erring Policy of the British Workingman" was published in *Cassier's Magazine* in 1901.[1] According to a well-known bibliographer, *Cassier's Magazine* was "One of the very best sources for ten-to-twenty page review articles of contemporary (engineering) practice" and was written for the intelligent engineer and informed general reader.[2]

Since the British workingman was very well organized, his attitude towards industrial changes not only affected the firm and trade but also the country.[3] Church was of the opinion that until some notion of a fair day's wage for a fair day's work came along, strife would be an ever present threat. Physical output standards were not enough.[4] He stated one of his central themes that "From that day on which intelligence came to the rescue of muscle, output began to be independent of rate of labour."[5] Hence, the worker was not entitled to all the fruits of increased output. He certainly sounded like an idealist.

> The workingman must grasp the simple truth that as long as man's daily work does not take him near the limit of physical or mental endurance, the amount of his output is, in reality, a matter of indifference to him in the personal sense. If, physically and mentally, his work is well within his powers; if, in the pecuniary sense, he is well up to the standard of comfort he is used to, any increased productiveness which improved methods have enabled his employer to arrange are so much clear gain, not to him personally, nor very often to his employer personally, but to the national industry in its power of competing successfully in the markets of the world.[6]

Furthermore, he also was quite optimistic, as he did not belong to the school of thought which held there was only so much work to do in the world.[7]

It's only fitting that, as an optimist eager for change, Church would turn toward America, the new hope for progressive change.[8] But one would be incorrect to assume that Church's optimism was devoid of practicality; on the contrary, nations which compensate their worker's output with high wage rates advance technologically and monetarily. Consequently, Church frequently harped upon the central theme that low wages were not necessarily good nor high wages necessarily bad. This point was made clear in the following quote about the issue of what country would get a contract for an order of new railway equipment.

> ...Who will stand the best chance of getting that order? Will it go to the country where the typical employer is he who pays the lowest wages, who has the least consideration for his men, who looks upon his business as a mill to grind out profits and dividends, and nothing else?
> It will not. It will go to that country, and no other, which has organised its business so that it has the largest output for the smallest expenditure. But this does not mean that the smallest rate of wages will be paid there. On the contrary, we have the example of America to show us that a high ratio of output to expenditure is always connected with a high wages-rate. The order will go to that country in which the artisans, as a body, not only "work new methods for all they are worth," but are eager to find out and adopt such methods. It will go to that country in which the artisans do not seek to handicap their employers by trying to make rates of wages independent of output, but base their claims for higher wages and more consideration on the only intelligible, and, in the long run, successful, basis,—higher efficiency in production per working day.[9]

He believed that if a new method of production displaced a worker, the productive capacity of the world had increased.[10] All the government measures in the world would not stop trade from flowing to the most efficient countries, which appeared to be Germany and the United States, rather than Great Britain.[11] He must have feared a recurrence of the Luddite riots.

> That they are not so realized is, however, perfectly plain. A Yorkshire engineer told the writer recently that amongst his employees, there is not only the bitterest antipathy exhibited towards new machines and new processes tending to increase output, but that this attitude is based up by a selfish cynicism that is the most saddening feature of the situation. "My men say that they will not do anything to increase output. It is nothing to them that business is lost. They tell me openly that when it goes elsewhere they will follow it."[12]

"The Future of Industry" was published in *The Unpopular Review* in June 1917. This magazine was a quarterly review published by Henry Holt and Company in New York. This journal is a difficult one to classify but it seemed to be oriented toward progressivism and against socialism.[13] In the article Church classified the 19th Century as the century of political democracy and the 20th Century as the century of economic democracy.[14] America was, once again, the focal point, although it was a political democracy but absolutist in terms of economic democracy.[15]

Church returned to the theme that the ever increasing size of organizations has spawned a science of organization. Yet, for one who seemed to be a free trader, he favored a moderation of competition.

> But unfortunately there is a third element in industry that is not yet brought under the reign of scientific law. While each productive unit in its internal structure is an example of coordinated activity, industry as a whole is still in the stage of being wholly uncoordinated, and is in fact a veritable scramble, very much as if in a factory, each new job were to be thrown on the floor and the whole body of workers invited to fight for its possession.[16]

Competition must be maintained but not necessarily in a full-blown manner. Why should ten firms in the same industry have to have ten different selling organizations? Why not divide the market and keep some plants from being idle? Church concluded that the resultant market monopoly would not be harmful if prices were not raised.[17]

Church went on then to propose a solution of consumer combines, which had worked in England.[18] He praised the agricultural combines of Denmark, Germany, and France, as well as the United States,[19] hoping that "The coordination of industry by the association of consumers, the free *association* of producers with free *access* to capital in proportion to capacity, the *averaging out* of the largest portion of human calamity by the agency of insurance, make a picture that is as yet far off from realization, but is at least commenced and sketched out."[20] The democratization of industry was evolving. Still, this evolution should not be forced but allowed to happen in the free play of the forces out there.[21]

He gave a broader setting for his philosophy of dealing with the ambition of man. This passage is quite similar to that of one in his 1923 book.

> To begin with, it is necessary to distinguish between the opportunity to rise and the opportunity to develop. While it is, of course, most important that the avenue to higher positions shall be kept open and made available as far as possible to members of the rank and file, it must be recognized that this alone is no solution of the problem. Though every private may carry a marshal's baton in his knapsack, it is obvious that very few can ever attain possession of that baton. The law of average in Human Faculty shows that the possession of capacity is comparatively rare, and no amount of education especially of the book-learning kind, can change the bearing of this law. The important part of the problem is the provision of opportunity for the rank and file to develop, quite apart from the rise of certain units out of it..[22]

Organized labor did not oppose men moving out of its ranks but opposed men in its ranks being rewarded more than others in its ranks. Church agreed that a form of group solidarity had to be maintained,[23] and he offered a more flexible, workable solution of group remuneration. This afforded a bridge "over which industry may pass by steady development from master-and-servant to more cooperative forms. Its hopefulness lies in the educative influence brought to bear on the ordinary man, and in the intensified economic value his services thus acquire, without separating him from his class."[24]

Church ended this writing with a paragraph which expressed his social philosophy.

> The true line of development is therefore seen to be some form of organization capable of being applied to existing productive units—since the form of organization obviously controls the direction of development—that will not merely allow, but foster, an increasing solidarity of interest between the workers as workers and the higher organization of industry. In this way alone can the eventual democratization of the economic relation be brought about. Such organization can only be developed by experiment, and in its experimental working out, it is important that both organized labor and the higher organization of industry shall be more mutually helpful and less mutually suspicious. That such a development can be successfully attained only by mutual cooperation, and not be paternalism, seems essentially true.[25]

The writer of this monograph found that the ideas from this section are quite global in nature and deal mostly with the worker and his trade unions. [Idea 105] Until some notion of a fair day's work for a fair day's wage come along, labor strife will continue. [Idea 106] Low wages are not necessarily good nor high wages necessarily bad. [Idea 107] When a new method of production replaces a worker, the productive capacity of the world increases. [Idea 108] All the government measures in the world would not stop trade from flowing to the most efficient countries. [Idea 109] Industry cooperation would tend to stabilize production amongst the firms. [Idea 110] A market monopoly which did not raise prices was not harmful. [Idea 111] Consumer combines can offset monopoly power. [Idea 112] Let the democratization of industry evolve. [Idea 113] The opportunity to rise out from the rank and file is not a solution to the class problem. [Idea 114] Paying men in the same rank more than others threatens group solidarity. [Idea 115] Mutual cooperation between management and trade unions must occur before mutual help can replace mutual suspicion.

There were no real surprises, except perhaps for the industry cooperation matter, in either of the two articles. Church was not sold on individual piecework system as the solution to the labor problems of the day. Labor was not entitled to all of the productivity gains. Workers must acquire a more global perspective and understand their role in the firm and in a prosperous society. Low wages were not necessarily the way to success but high productivity was.

83

By 1917, Church had taken a more visionary perspective. It is interesting to note his willingness to modify, but not destroy, the competitive model to smooth out production within the firms. Idle machines never left his mind. Church's cooperatives probably never had quite the effects he imagined in the United States but his notion of an evolutionary movement to industrial democracy seemed to have been accurate. One aspect of his writings which needs new and empirical research is his group bonus system. His rationale for this wage payment plan may need to be revisited today. His various writings on this topic need to be put into an holistic framework and tested empirically. He may have been right.

Industrial Engineering
1913, 1915, 1922, and 1927

Church also published works of a much more specific nature in comparing and contrasting wage incentive systems in 1913, in describing the design function in 1915, and then plant layout issues in 1922 and 1927, springing from his long association with the Mount Hope Finishing Company. These seven articles give another perspective of Church.

In the October and November, 1913 issues of *The Engineering Magazine*, Church published a two-part series of "Premium, Piecework, and the Expense Burden,"[26] and "Bonus Systems and the Expense Burden."[27] These articles had been written some years prior to 1913 but had been put on the "back-burner" by Church when he switched his interest to more comprehensive considerations of schools, systems, and principles of management.[28] Still, as we see with this opening discussion on what costs should be attached to the product, we soon realize that Church retained his in-depth, analytical style even when discussing the nitty gritty aspects of production. "When, however, we recognize that indirect expenses are passing minute by minute into the real cost of an article under process of manufacture, we not only widen our point of view in a very useful way, but are able to grasp more clearly the economic status of piece work and premium.[29] Many times the only benefit to the employer from an increase in production was this decrease in burden per unit.[30]

Church labeled piecework nothing more than 100 percent premium work.[31] Employers had two practical instincts in a wage payment system. The first was that "The expense burden has a vital connection with the question, and that an actual reduction in time taken means a reduced total or works cost, though it does not mean a reduction in wages cost."[32] The second was that "After a certain point is reached, excessive earnings on the part of the man are out of proportion to the benefit from reduction in burden realized by the employer."[33] Piecework would result in halving total costs until the burden rate is 160 percent or higher.[34] "The higher the burden, the sharper is the fall of the works-cost line relative to wages, as cost is reduced."[35]

He then detailed four wage payment systems: (1) the 100 percent piecework system; (2) the Halsey system at 50 percent; (3) the Halsey system at 33⅓ percent, and (4) the Rowan system.[36] Many graphs were presented.[37] All four systems indicated that a low rate of burden should call for a low rate of premium.[38] The results of an incentive system should not be to enable workmen to double pay but to allow: "(1) incentive to increase production at the right moment and under the right conditions; and (2) a just and equitable distribution of the savings effected."[39] Church favored the Rowan system, which increased the worker's pay proportionate to the reduction of the time allowances.[40] "It says, in effect, that if he reduces time 25 percent or 50 percent, his pay shall be increased 25 percent or 50 percent or whatever other fractional reduction of time he affects."[41] The Rowan system offered its greatest degree of incentives for moderate cost reductions and did not permit such anomolies as a five-fold increase in pay.[42] He concluded:

> Of the four systems examined, the Rowan system seems to prevent, in practice, any arrival at a point where the interests of employer and employee come into actual conflict. It either produces or fails to produce sufficiently satisfactory economic results. In neither case does anybody lose; they only fail to gain. There is a psychological difference in that

which has important practical bearings, and makes for industrial peace. And a remedy can generally be found, where interest do not drift into antagonism at any stage of their relations.[43]

The second article discussed two different bonus approaches, the Gantt Bonus method and the Emerson Efficiency Method.[44] Both these methods were the result of the revolutionary movement of determining a theoretical maximum of productive output.[45] Church very much feared the danger of declining piecework rates on employee morale. Competition would force this happening, even though one company might hold firm for a while. He offered this hope.

> Up to the present time all systems of piece remuneration must be considered as temporary and practical solutions of a problem of great importance—involving a certain amount of dissatisfaction at times, but kept working by the common-sense and fair dealing of the parties to the bargain. The special interest of the task and bonus methods is that they are a considerable step forward towards a state of affairs when most piece-work prices will be referred to an ultimate or real basis and thus be beyond dispute, either at different times in the same shop, or at the same period in different shops; not because of the peculiar methods by which payment is reckoned, but on account of their minute survey of the maximum possible production, and their enumeration of every factor occurring in such production.[46]

The Gantt method was described as follows:

> ...In the Gantt method a time limit, or allowance, is set as in all other methods of payment by results; and precisely as in ordinary piece work, any reduction of this limit goes entirely into the pocket of the worker. But in addition to this, a bonus of 20 to 40 percent on the time actually spent on the job is paid to him if, and only if, he succeeds in attaining or reducing the time limit. In all other systems hitherto examined, the passage from day pay to extra earnings is smooth and gradual. Whatever premium or reward is paid to the worker is given for reduction of a time limit, and is in strict proportion to the amount of that reduction. The only difference between those systems is in the relation of the reward of extra effort to the total works cost of the job.[47]

Church praised the psychological effect of the Gantt method, which highlighted incompetence in the holding back of progress toward a definite and ascertained goal.[48] "It is an ineradicable factor of human nature to struggle toward a definite ideal—the real trouble of life being that few of us get hold of the right ideal. This applies quite as much in the prosaic atmosphere of the machine shop as anywhere else...."[49] He then made quite an attribution to the Gantt system.

> But no one who is familiar with the question can fail to perceive that the new view of production given by Mr. Gantt lies in the same straight line with the "production-factor" method of dealing with expense burden advocated by the present writer. In wholly independent fields they both tend towards the same end, and that is the predetermination of theoretical efficiency. The tendency in both is to consider each machine as a "production centre" and thoroughly to discuss, enumerate and record all the conditions of its maximum successful operation. They both seek to set up definite standards of work, by which the efficiency of all similar machines wherever placed can be judged.[50]

Church considered the Emerson system to be nothing more than a 66 percent Halsey limit.[51] Church did not give a definite answer as to which of the two systems, Gantt's or Emerson's, would be better without an analysis of the factors involved in a given situation. He did generally favor the Gantt standard as it seemed to offer a greater leverage on average human nature than the gradual rise of earnings on the Emerson method.[52] Once again, the bonus approach was related to burden.

> For if we assume a standard task and agree to regard any failure to perform, it is evident that we imply a standard quantity of burden, whether the latter is regarded as a percentage of time, or wages, or is treated on the "production-centre" system of machine rents. There is, then, a double degree of inefficiency in failure to come up to standard on any job. Not

only is there a loss of time, but what is sometimes even more important, there is an undue absorption of burden. The modern principle of predetermination of standard time-cost requires to be supplemented by similar standardization of overhead burden, in order to bring all the elements of cost to a focus.[53]

A letter from Church to the editor of the *American Machinist* on June 20, 1915, entitled "The Evolution of Design,"[54] contained his opinions on an article written by Kimball.[55] Church agreed with Kimball that there was a dawning of a new and more perfect sense of fitness, perhaps due to the great triumphs of modern scientific invention.[56] In fact, Church was quite willing to rank the sight of a collection of chemical apparatus as intellectually pleasurable as a contemplation of the Sistine Madonna.[57]

Church published a short article, "Machine Design and the Design of Systems," in 1915, in which he did a nice job of comparing and contrasting these two uses of the design function. He wrote:

> ...A badly designed machine will either not work at all or, by comparison with some other machine, can be seen to be inferior; but a badly designed system always works after a fashion, and the opportunities for comparing it with *what might have been* hardly exists at all.[58]

There is no finality in machine design and there are a number of experts always on hand with updated knowledge.[59] A good machine does not have to be discarded until the new experimental model has been tried.[60] This is not true with a management control system. Most firms do not have a management organization expert on hand.[61] What works at one place may not necessarily work at the next.[62] The changes in a managerial organization are a much more serious matter than experimenting with new elements in a machine.[63] Hence, Church concluded that management changes should not be done by the non-expert.[64]

Church published a two-part series in 1922 issues of *Management Engineering* on his experiences at the Mount Hope Finishing Company.[65] The Mount Hope plant had grown rapidly and was experiencing intercommunication problems between departments. He described the "cross-iron" method of connecting trailers.[66] Great detail was given about the logic and layout of the storage area, which was "laid out in numbered spaces, each space being the size of a skid, and every space has a skid belonging to it *bearing its number.*"[67] The result of the new system was that one man with a forklift and two indirect laborers could do more work than 15 men had previously done.[68] He further explained his theory of the Mount Hope Finishing work in 1927.[69] He started by explaining the trade off between the factors of ease of handling and space.

> Nearly every improvement or new degree of efficiency in industrial engineering has to be purchased at price. Minimum handling cannot be effected in crowded spaces without the employment of specially designed and complex machinery; not always then. In the case the price is obvious and usually a heavy one. On the other hand the price of efficient handling on the tractor system is adequate space... [70]

He recommended the preparation of a larger scale plan of the plant and on that plan a flow diagram of material movements shown by lines drawn proportionately in thickness to the volume of goods passing between any two points.[71] The runway system adopted must be a compromise between the handling and space factors present.[72] He recommended elevators for consideration only in multi-story buildings.[73] Compromise dictated a combination of hand and machine methods.[74] He ended with a call for cooperation between architects, construction engineers, and industrial engineers when the plant is being designed.[75]

The writer of this monograph found that the first set of ideas centered on employee compensation methods. [Idea 116] The decrease in burden per unit is a key factor in adopting worker incentive method. [Idea 117] Unless care is exercised by management, an employee incentive method can lead to much more benefits for the worker than for the firm. [Idea 118] When the burden rate is low, the premium should also be at a low rate. [Idea 119] The interests of the employer and the employee in a wage incentive system must not conflict. [Idea 120] There will be a time when the ultimate efficiency will be known and then piece-work controversies will go away.

The second set of ideas were based on the topic of transportation within the plant. [Idea 121] Numbered spaces and numbered skids must be matched. [Idea 122] There is a trade-off between ease of handling and space. [Idea 123] Minimum handling cannot be affected in crowded spaces without the employment of specially designed and complex machinery, if possible at all. [Idea 124] There should be a large scale plan of the plant with a flow diagram of material movements on the plan. [Idea 125] There should be cooperation between architects, construction engineers, and industrial engineers while the plant is being designed.

There were no surprises in this section. While Church may never had put all his writings and philosophies together in one effort on paper, he certainly had his ideas together in his mind. The dangers of 1200 percent piecework were again stressed, as was his life-long concerns with burden and low wages. He wasn't afraid to go into great detail with graphs and he was willing to make general endorsements of the Rowan system and then the Gantt Bonus Method. Both had certain psychological advantages, especially Gantt's delineation of the ideal. While the articles about his Mount Hope experiences tended to the specific, Church still generalized specifics into principles.

CHAPTER SEVEN
CONCLUSIONS

As you probably recall, this writer explained the eight reasons why this monograph was written. In this concluding chapter, these reasons are reviewed again in light of the material presented in Chapters Two through Six. Consequently, the writer's final comments are covered under these topic headings: (1) ideas of Church; (2) was Church a classic forerunner of a management accountant?; (3) gaps and possible misinterpretations in Church's background; (4) relationships of Church with the early pioneers of management; (5) an holistic view of Church's writings; (6) case studies of Church's systems in management accounting; (7) engineering input into management and accounting; and (8) scientific management and Church. The last section discusses the avenues open to any researcher interested in pursuing the still inconclusive findings on Church's life and works.

Ideas of Church

The 125 ideas taken from Church's writings by the writer are placed in a chart in numerical order. They are ranked on a 5 point scale for originality, value then, value now, and value in the future with 1 being "extremely significant" and 5 being "insignificant." (See Figure 10.) These rankings are obviously subjective and the readers are invited to come up with their own rankings. Only ideas that received a ranking of 1 in each of the four rankings are discussed in this section. These ideas are grouped, in turn, into five segments: (1) machinery and overhead; (2) idle time and waste; (3) principles and uniqueness; (4) worker and foreman; and (5) distribution costs and expansion policies. Be that as it may, the chart of ideas gives a very good summary of Church's writings and is a vivid reminder that he was a man of action trying to solve problems as well as a contemplator.

The first grouping of ideas come from Church's first efforts and deal with machinery and overhead. The most important idea of all, in the writer's opinion, was (2) "The machine-hour rate method is a far superior method of accounting for overhead in a highly capital intensive firm than other methods of overhead accounting." The writer was thus attracted initially to Church because of this idea and this writer remains convinced that accounting is 200 years behind the times by not having a wide-spread adoption of the machine-hour rate method, especially in the era of robotics. Church had foresight, then, and creativity. His lucid writing style led to such masterful pieces as the little shop analogy, the example which allowed Church to arrive at idea (3), "The production center is the lowest level of collection of accounting data and might be just one machine." This idea unshackles the notion that accounting for machinery must be bound by departments. (4) "The machine should

Figure 10
Ideas of Church

	Ideas	Originality	Value		
			Then	Now	Future
(1)	Overhead is a product cost.	2	2	2	1
(2)	The machine-hour rate method is a far superior method of accounting for overhead in a highly capital-intensive firm than other methods of overhead accounting.	1	1	1	1 *
(3)	The production center is the lowest level of collection of accounting data and might be just one machine.	1	1	1	1 *
(4)	The machine should be the focal point of management efforts.	1	1	1	1 *
(5)	Accounting is a vital part of managerial control.	2	1	1	1
(6)	All costs should be recorded, allocated to jobs, and be recovered in the selling price.	2	1	1	1
(7)	Imputed interest on capital is an overhead cost to the firm.	1	1	1	1 *
(8)	Direct labor approaches to overhead allocation are disastrous	1	1	1	1 *
(9)	Overhead is growing, while direct labor costs are shrinking.	1	1	1	1 *
(10)	Machines must not be idle.	1	1	1	1 *
(11)	Accounting should immediately highlight idle machines, and, hence, idle capacity.	1	1	1	1 *
(12)	There are many factors of production.	1	1	1	1 *
(13)	Overhead must be analyzed by factors of production.	1	1	1	1 *
(14)	There should be a comparison of actual costs to standard costs.	5	1	1	1
(15)	Overtime must be controlled.	2	2	2	2
(16)	Fixed/variable analysis is extremely helpful in controlling overhead.	3	2	2	2
(17)	There are principles of overhead treatment.	1	2	1	1
(18)	The techniques of applying the principles of overhead are going to vary with the situation at hand.	•2	2	2	2
(19)	Overhead is the cost of capacity to produce.	1	1	1	1 *
(20)	The cost of capital should be broadly based.	3	3	3	3
(21)	The accountant has to be as vitally involved in issues of waste, spoilage, scrap, and by-products as he is in accounting for utilization of machinery.	1	1	1	1 *
(22)	Work being performed in the plant must be controlled by a detailed job and production order system.	3	2	2	2
(23)	One must take account of the timing of expenses in passing judgment on management performances for a given time period.	5	3	3	3
(24)	The six factors of production are machinery, organization, supervision, stores transport, power, and space.	1	2	3	3
(25)	What happens when the last direct laborer is gone from the plant?	1	2	1	1
(26)	All catastrophies and accidental items should be excluded from overhead.	4	2	2	2
(27)	Budgeting mandated the service-factor calculations.	3	3	3	3
(28)	Standards should be changed whenever any element of direct cost is no longer identical with its corresponding item in the standard cost card.	3	3	3	3
(29)	Standards must be checked against actual accounting data.	2	1	1	1
(30)	While management must know the profit from each job, they should not disclose this in financial accounting reports because of the many suppositions going into this profit calculation.	1	3	3	3

Figure 10 (continued)

Ideas	Originality	Value Then	Value Now	Value Future
(31) Revaluations of property for financial accounting purposes should not be given effect in the cost accounting records because of internal comparison purposes.	4	3	1	1
(32) Direct labor might be merged with overhead costs to get a single processing rate.	2	4	4	4
(33) A constant amount of a total of depreciation and interest provides the best figure for cost planning purposes.	3	2	1	1
(34) It is possible to find a rational basis for allocating factors such as storage-transport, supervision, and organization.	2	2	2	2
(35) Management may use the machine-hour rate concept as a "super rate" to analyze its current allocation method and its operating efficiency.	1	1	1	1 *
(36) The manufacturing world had entered an extremely more complex arena.	3	2	2	2
(37) The control system for an organization is as needed as and similar in function to the nervous system of a person.	1	1	1	1 *
(38) The control system must replace the master's eyes and brains in the daily progress of work.	1	2	2	2
(39) The increasing threat of competition has caused the need for complex control systems to coordinate the many parts of the organization.	2	2	2	2
(40) Each business is different and local needs must be met within the framework of overall principles.	1	1	1	1 *
(41) Prime costs are not enough to know.	1	1	1	1 *
(42) The accounting staff should be in a centralized location.	2	2	2	2
(43) A continuous stock-taking system is necessary to arrive at the needed accounting statements.	3	2	2	2
(44) The United States is where to look for progress in manufacturing.	2	1	2	3
(45) Scientific management is a body of principles and not a system. These principles may be applied in a great variety of ways, as long as the principles are kept.	1	1	1	1 *
(46) Scientific management has not settled the warring claims of capital and labor.	1	1	2	2
(47) The following of the principles of management will lead to a greater pot to be shared by employees.	2	2	2	2
(48) Labor is not the creator of all wealth.	2	2	2	2
(49) Change should be evolutionary, not revolutionary.	1	1	1	1 *
(50) The role of the foreman is to provide elasticity of reactions to current events within the rigidity of the organization.	1	1	1	1 *
(51) The foreman represents the last outpost of general control and is the master's eyes for that department.	1	1	2	3
(52) The three principles of management are:(1) the systematic use of experience; (2) the economic control of effort; and (3) the promotion of personal effectiveness.	1	1	1	1 *
(53) The systematic use of experience is the careful analysis of what is about to be attempted and its reference to existing records and standards of performance.	2	2	2	2
(54) A "square deal" is needed for workers.	2	2	2	2
(55) Leadership is probably the most important part of a fine work atmosphere.	2	2	2	2
(56) Good work habits should be created for all.	1	1	1	1 *
(57) Management is concerned with "analysis" and "synthesis"--the constructive instrument which builds.	2	2	2	2

91

Figure 10 (continued)

Ideas	Originality	Then	Now	Future
(58) "Analysis" focuses on cost accounting, which records and compares the money value of each of the very small steps in the production process.	2	1	2	1
(59) "Synthesis" is the choice, the relative effectiveness, the right proportion, the right kind of means that is in question.	1	1	1	1 *
(60) The five organic functions of management are design, equipment, control, comparison, and operation.	1	1	2	1
(61) Control fixes the relations of persons throughout the plant and selects the right personalities to fill these posts.	2	2	2	2
(62) The goal of comparison is to substitute quantitative for qualitative measurement methods.	2	1	1	1
(63) Accounting must be concerned with efficiencies measured in time, numbers, and weight, as well as in dollars.	1	1	1	1 *
(64) Accounting should not be governed by mechanical appliances, in that the work has been fitted to the machine rather than the machine used as an aid to indispensable work.	1	3	2	1
(65) Results of operations must be controlled and safeguarded by a thoroughly modern accounting system.	2	2	2	2
(66) Records of waste must be tied into the general accounting system.	1	1	1	1 *
(67) A job should be analyzed to determine the special human faculty concerned.	2	2	2	1 *
(68) Tests should be used to determine the faculties of the job applicants.	2	2	2	2
(69) Esprit de corps must be fostered.	1	1	1	1 *
(70) The technique of time study should best be conducted off the shop floor and be the basis for establishing new and better work habits.	1	1	1	1 *
(71) Men will manipulate their behavior to give the appearance of doing well.	1	1	1	1 *
(72) Incentive systems should call out the full use of the talents of that particular grade of worker.	1	1	2	3
(73) The group bonus system can enhance group pride.	1	1	1	1 *
(74) Workers need to have confidence in the records of the firm in the computation of the group bonus.	1	1	1	1 *
(75) Time study must take into account the gains in skill in doing a long repeated job.	1	1	1	1 *
(76) Each kind of equipment must be present in the right proportion and in the right quantity.	2	2	2	2
(77) Each department must be allocated the proportional amount of space fitted to its needs.	2	2	2	2
(78) Expansion to meet new business must be planned.	1	1	1	1 *
(79) There should be a Book of the Plant.	2	2	2	2
(80) Equipment must be arranged so that product, persons and communications follow the path of least effort.	2	1	1	1
(81) There should be an idle time chart for machinery.	1	1	1	1 *
(82) The foreman must have exceptional matters brought to his attention.	1	1	1	1 *
(83) Immediate recording is needed for immediate discussions to be held. Detail must be piping-hot. The people who make the detail are the people who can use the detail.	2	1	1	1
(84) There should be a master schedule which controls all the sequences of work done.	2	1	1	1
(85) Budget/actual comparisons should be made.	3	1	1	1

Figure 10 (continued)

	Ideas	Originality	Value Then	Value Now	Value Future
(86)	Commercial wastes and by-products must be better marketed.	1	1	1	1*
(87)	To insure competitiveness, the executive must continually be on the search for new ideas, new machinery, and new methods.	2	1	1	1
(88)	Selling costs and office costs are to be analyzed in many different ways, including unit costs.	1	1	1	1*
(89)	A customer on the books should be a permanent asset to the business.	1	1	1	1*
(90)	Every complaint must be analyzed by one official or one department.	2	1	2	2
(91)	Specialized machines should not be installed unless there is practical assurance that they can be kept working to their full capacity.	1	1	1	1*
(92)	The executive should seek or accept business for which the plant is perfectly fitted.	2	2	2	2
(93)	The product, even machinery, should have a good appearance.	2	1	1	1
(94)	The cost of a thing made is a very different matter from the cost of the same thing sold.	1	1	1	1*
(95)	The selling function must be routinized by use of a sales manual and by a careful layout of sales routes.	2	2	2	2
(96)	The sales forecast is crucial.	2	2	2	2
(97)	A technical library and information system must be established.	1	1	1	1*
(98)	Vagueness of all kinds is one of the great business pitfalls.	2	1	1	1*
(99)	Meters and recorders, as well as calculating and statistical machines, must be known by the executive.	1	1	1	1*
(100)	The amount of liability for outstanding purchase orders must be known by the executive.	1 •	1	1	1*
(101)	The executive must balance the three factors of successful purchasing.	2	2	2	2*
(102)	There should be a purchase-order control board.	2	2	2	2
(103)	A card system should be established for each worker.	2	2	2	2
(104)	Employee committees lead to better decisions for employee social expenditures than paternalism.	1	1	1	1*
(105)	Until some notion of a fair day's work for a fair day's wage comes along, labor strife will continue.	1	1	2	2
(106)	Low wages are not necessarily good nor high wages necessarily bad.	1	1	1	1*
(107)	When a new method of production replaces a worker, the productive capacity of the world increases.	2	2	2	2
(108)	All the government measures in the world would not stop trade from flowing to the most efficient countries.	4	1	1	1*
(109)	Industry cooperation would tend to stabilize production amongst the firms.	2	1	2	2
(110)	A market monopoly which did not raise prices was not harmful.	3	3	3	3
(111)	Consumer combines can offset monopoly power.	2	2	2	2
(112)	Let the democratization of industry evolve.	1	2	1	1
(113)	The opportunity to rise out from the rank and file is not a solution to the class problem.	1	1	2	2

Figure 10 (continued)

Ideas	Originality	Value		
		Then	Now	Future
(114) Paying men in the same rank more than others threatens group solidarity.	2	1	1	1
(115) Mutual cooperation between management and trade unions must occur before mutual help can replace mutual suspicion.	2	2	1	2
(116) The decrease in burden per unit is a key factor in adopting a worker incentive method.	1	1	2	3
(117) Unless care is exercised by management, an employee incentive method can lead to much more benefits for the worker than for the firm.	1	1	2	3
(118) When the burden rate is low, the premium should also be at a low rate.	1	1	2	3
(119) The interests of the employee and the employer in a wage incentive system must not conflict.	1	1	2	3
(120) There will be a time when the ultimate efficiency will be known and then piecework controversies will go away.	2	2	3	4
(121) Numbered spaces and numbered skids must be matched.	2	2	2	2
(122) There is a trade-off between ease of handling and space.	2	2	2	2
(123) Minimum handling cannot be affected in crowded spaces without the employment of specially designed and complex machinery, if possible at all.	2	2	2	2
(124) There should be a large scale plan of the plant with a flow diagram of material movements on the plan.	2	1	2	2
(125) There should be cooperation between architects, construction engineers, and industrial engineers while the plant is being designed.	1	1	1	1 *

be the focal point of management efforts" flows from ideas (2) and (3). (7) "Imputed interest on capital is an overhead cost to the firm" illustrates the expansive notion that Church had of cost and his willingness to be free of the financial accounting model.

There should be, in the writer's opinion, a motto over the desk of all those concerned with manufacturing accounting and that is (8) "Direct labor approaches to overhead allocation are disastrous." This is even more poignant as (9) "Overhead is growing, while direct labor costs are shrinking." What will happen when the last direct laborer leaves a firm? How will accounting survive?

Church really had a second thrust in overhead accounting and that was (12) "There are many factors of production," and (13) "Overhead must be analyzed by factors of production." These ideas not only deepened the machine-hour-rate method and made it more understandable but could have been the basis for much further development by him. It may well be that accounting should adopt a more than four-pronged cost classification system—i.e., direct labor, direct material, machinery, and overhead. Church, at least, brought out the fourth prong of machinery but there could be firms which would receive better information with a five, six, or seven prong product cost system with such classifications as research and development, quality control, and/or employee relations.

(41) "Prime costs are not enough to know" follows from the notion of concern about overhead. Church apparently never was involved, or at least just passingly, with direct costers and the direct costing issue. (19) "Overhead is the cost of capacity to produce" justified the allocation of overhead in a rational manner. This writer once was a "direct coster" but has come to the conclusion that the direct cost approach is inappropriate for a highly capital-intensive firm.

The use of the machine hour rate as an "off-the-ledger" control tool was recommended by (35) "Management may use the machine-hour rate concept as a 'super rate' to analyze its current allocation method and its operating efficiency." This willingness to leave the "on the ledger" system marked quite a change for Church.

Church was at his most clairvoyant on (99) "Meters and records, as well as calculating and statistical machines, must be known by the executive." His writings and systems would have been much better received if they were written now, because of the explosion of knowledge and machinery in these areas. He wrote just in the beginning of the counting devices and made himself heard. The writer is convinced that Church's writings and systems should be re-examined in the light of both current and future technologies in the measurement area.

The second grouping of ideas are somewhat related to the first grouping and deal with idle time and waste. Both these topics represented arenas in which management could do much better and would do it better, if they only knew the lost dollars involved. (10) "Machines must not be idle," and (11) "Accounting should immediately highlight idle machines, and, hence, idle capacity" flow from Church's overriding concern about the management of machinery. Idle time represented "waste" in his later writings and "waste" was expanded into the area of material as well as time. (21) "The accountant has to be as vitally involved in issues of waste, spoilage, scrap, and by-products as he is in accounting for utilization of machinery." Dollars were not to be the only measurement amount in accounting, because (63) "Accounting must be concerned with efficiencies in time, number, and weight, as well as in dollars." (66) "Records of waste must be tied into the general accounting system." As one might expect knowing Church's proclivity for visual aids, (81) "There should be an idle time chart for machinery." The last idea in this grouping dealt with waste from a more deterministic management viewpoint. (86) "Commercial wastes and by-products must be better marketed."

The third grouping of ideas centered around the principles and uniqueness topics. These views were markedly different from that of the "Taylorites," "systemitizers," and "scientific managers," at least as established in Church's strawmen. (40) "Each business is different and local needs must be met within the framework of overall principles." (45) "Scientific management is a body of principles and not a system. The principles may be applied in a great variety of ways, as long as the principles are kept." Church wanted change to spring from the current work group and not be imposed on it by outsiders employing methods that might have worked in their last consulting job. (49) "Change should be evolutionary, not revolutionary."

These principles were articulated and placed in a logically-tight system. (37) "The control system for an organization is as needed as and similar in function to the nervous system of a person." (52) "The three principles of management are: (1) the systematic use of experience; (2) the economic control of effort; and (3) the promotion of personal effectiveness." Management was to synthesize, as well as analyze. (59) "Synthesis' is the choice, the relative effectiveness, the right proportion, the right kind of means that is in question." Church continued to stress the leader and the leadership role as the most crucial to the work atmosphere of a company. (69) *Espirit de corps* must be fostered."

The fourth grouping of ideas concerned workers and foremen and illustrate Church's ability to be concerned with both global and specific sides of an issue. His interests in foremen are especially interesting to the writer, as Church could be labeled as the Champion of Foremen. (49) "Change should be evolutionary, not revolutionary." This gave workers and foremen the opportunity to be involved with and accustomed to change. (50) "The role of the foreman is to provide elasticity of reactions to current events within the rigidity of the organization."

Church was an optimist in his outlook towards workers, as long as they weren't square pegs in a round hole. (56) "Good work habits should be created for all." It was to be with the role of creating good work habits that time study should play its major part. (70) "The technique of time study should best be conducted off the shop floor and be the basis for establishing new and better work habits." However, Church was more cautious about the use of the field of psychology to develop good habits. (71) "Men will manipulate their behavior to give the appearance of doing well."

He did propose a solution for the inadequacies of some, if not most, of the piecework wage incentive systems. (73) "The group bonus system can enhance group pride." (74) "Workers need to have confidence in the records of the firm in the computation of the group bonus." Church had another concern about a familiar sore point. (75) "Time study must take into account the gains in skill in doing a long repeated job." This is a premonition of the learning-curve phenomena finding.

The last three ideas in this grouping are consistent with his positive views of the importance of both foremen and workers. (82) "The foreman must have exceptional matters brought to his attention." Church considered foremen to be a key focal point of a reporting system. He also had much more faith in the workers' choosing their own employee programs than the employer so doing. (104) "Employee committees lead to better decisions for employee social expenditures than paternalism." The last item was a central theme of his. (106) "Low wages are not necessarily good nor high wages necessarily bad."

The last of the groupings of ideas were distribution costs and expansion policies. Church was quite cautious about the effects of accepting new business. (78) "Expansion to meet new business must be planned." Perhaps expansion efforts should be focused on wastes. (86) "Commercial wastes and by-products must be better marketed." These marketing costs must be controlled. (88) "Selling costs and office costs are to be analyzed in many different ways, including unit costs." The worth of a customer must be known. (89) "A customer on the books should be a permanent asset to the business." A corollary to (78) is (91). "Specialized machines should not be installed unless there is practical assurance that they can be kept working to their full capacity." A corollary to (91) is (94). "The cost of a thing *made* is a very different matter from the cost of the same thing *sold*."

There were ways to attain technical betterments. (97) "A technical library and information system must be established." Church was concerned with the dangers of out-of-control purchase commitments. (100) "The amount of liability for outstanding purchase orders must be known by the executive." Lastly, Church gave another example of his concern with coordination and cooperation in the designing stage. (125) "There should be cooperation between architects, construction engineers, and industrial engineers while the plant is being designed."

Was Church a Classic Forerunner of a Management Accountant?

There is no doubt that Church was a formidable forerunner in the fields of management and of accounting. He stood out in both fields. Can one just put the words "management" and "accountant" together and then conclude that Church was a "management accountant"? While Church's writings in management were both specific and general, were his writings in accounting too oriented towards the specifics of cost accounting for the broader picture of financial accounting? Would he have been pleased with the appellation of "management accountant" applied to him?

One of the most telling reasons not to list Church as a classic forerunner of a management accountant was his decision not to employ the traditional approach to journalization. It seems that he used every means possible to avoid the straight debit/credit approach. Garner criticized the 1908 book on this score, when he wrote that Church neglected to give much attention to the ledger treatment.[1] Garner also criticized the 1917 book for using a roundabout method for securing the desired control without really using the control account device. In the same manner, Kimball mentioned that the 1917 book did not discuss the primary principles and mechanisms of cost finding in as complete a manner as other cost books. Cameron likewise questioned the wisdom of Church's attempting to teach or explain the theory of double entry in the small part of the 1917 book devoted to it.[4] Greely joined in this criticism.[5]

This reviewer remains somewhat puzzled about Church's carelessness, or perhaps lack of interest, in this rather basic issue of debits and credits. Perhaps Church was determined not to "sink to the level of a bookkeeper." This explanation is, in the writer's opinion, probably the most accurate of the three. It doesn't square with Church's concern about the worker and the foreman, in that the bookkeeper is at the lowest level in the accounting pecking order. However, it does square with his negativism about "commercial accountants." For whatever reason or reasons, Church committed a serious error by not using the best means of communication in accounting—the journal entry. One would expect a classic forerunner of management accounting to make better use of the accounting language than this.

Even more telling that the debit/credit issue is the topic of Church's disdain for "commercial accounting" and "commercial accountants." Some of this disdain could be labeled as rhetorical but clearly not most of it. In his 1908 book he stated that the mischief was already done by the time commercial accountants made their report [6] and that "figures will prove anything, 'except facts.'"[7] In 1910 he wrote "The accountant is concerned neither with efficiency nor the improvement of production."[8] In his 1917 preface, Church related that the cost man was not as appreciative about the role of the general accountant as he might be. Church in his 1923 book defined the role of financial accountants as being "concerned with the verification of cash and balance sheets..."[10] Coupled with this disdain was a sense of neglect; Church seemingly did not know certain accounting terms. For instance, Coffman complained that Church did not in the 1929 revision use up-to-date accounting terminology.[11] Church's attempt at exploring the difference between "profit" and "surplus" in his 1923 book is an example of that.[12] Whether it be rhetoric, be disdain, or be ignorance, Church in the writer's opinion, committed a serious faux pas by not communicating better with financial accountants or caring enough about financial accounting. Much wasted effort and emotions could have been saved on such issues as the supplementary rate, the idle capacity charge, and the imputation of interest, if Church had the proper amount of empathy for financial accountants. Clearly one would expect a forerunner of the management accountant to do better than this.

The next point is Church's seeming preference to complexity over simplicity, especially in his early machine-hour rate system. Sir Charles Renold reported that the Church system at Renold Ltd. became quite unmanageable in its ramifications, elaborations, and adjustments.[13] Roland Dunkerley reported the impracticality of many of Church's statements and teachings.[14] And Galloway cited the impracticality of Church's suggestion that actual costs be determined in such minute detail.[15] Three quotes from Church give great insight into his concerns. "...The snare of the 'simple system' must therefore be avoided..."[16] "...*No facts that are in themselves complex can be represented in fewer elements than they naturally possess...*"[17] "The cost man is rarely an accountant in the full sense of that word. He lives in a world of detail..."[18] This reviewer is of the opinion that modern data processing machinery would have solved many of the problems with the Church system at the Renold Company. However, it is fairly clear that Church's system and writings would have benefited from a loosening of his concern for detail. It is unlikely that some of the detail passed the cost/benefit test, at least in the early 1900's. He wouldn't have passed on the information overload test either. Clearly, Church was not a forerunner of the cost/benefit analysis of information collected and hence he most likely failed this test of the management accountant.

However, there are two significant instances in which Church certainly was a trailblazer for the management accountant. One instance was his excellent use of charts, graphs, and other visual aids. His works abound with these fine performances. The second from his 1914 book was his broad view of what information the accountant should collect. "...Accounting *in its broadest sense is the practical application of the science of quantities. It measures and records, not merely cash, but every kind of quantity that is concerned in the processes of a business. ...*"[19] Church not only would have been a forerunner in his times with these two examples but would now be significantly ahead of most management accountants today on these two topics.

Nevertheless, the writer is forced to the conclusion that Church should not be labeled as a forerunner of a management accountant. It is somewhat tragic to conclude that, because one would expect a pathfinder in accounting and in management to be able to be a pathfinder in management accounting. This is even more true with his excellent use of visual presentations and his broad view of accounting data collection. However, Church immeasurably damaged himself by his failure to use the traditional journal entry format, by his abuse and/or ignorance and/or lack of empathy for financial accountants and financial accounting, and by his seeming overconcern with detail. Any refinements of his efforts in accounting must come to grips with these failings, especially the financial accounting issue. Changes made in internal accounting must be considered in the light of their financial accounting portrayal. If Church had followed this maxim, his work would have had a much greater impact then and would not have been relegated to the dusty part of a library shelf. This writer especially laments Church's failure to smash the three product cost model (raw materials, direct labor, and overhead) at the turn of the century. The writer believes this basic model is flawed and that if Church were more involved with accounting nicities, he would have added at least a fourth product cost, machine labor, to the traditional model.

Gaps and Possible Misinterpretations
in Church's Background

While gaps in Church's resume do intrigue one to fill them and add a bit of mystery which enlivens a biography, ultimately these gaps cause frustration and surrender and seriously limit the study of his works. The writer has spent countless days in quest for more information about Church and understands why previous reviewers of Church had been totally frustrated by all sorts of roadblocks. This writer makes no criticisms of any of the past reviewers of Church and only thanks them for the efforts they made.

Church's place of birth most likely was near London, England. It is conceivable a review of each of the towns near London might yield a birth certificate. The writer was back in the United States, when he learned of this, so he has not searched the vital records in London for this information. The specifics of Church's education remain unclear, even though he was reported to have received a liberal education.[20] Oxford University, at which Urwick listed that Church might have attended, had no record of Church.[21] Whether Church was a technical expert and works manager in an electrical manufacturing business[22] or was an electrical engineer[23] is unclear. It is unfortunate that Church's academic background is so enshrouded in mystery, for his academic background would give an interesting clue as from what books and teachers might have inspired him. He was clearly a well read and erudite man with broad social interest. The writer thinks there is more likelihood that Church's education was more liberal than technical.

It is interesting to note the tie-in between Leonard Massey, Joseph Bell, and Hans Renold, all in the Manchester area. Manchester was a hotbed of manufacturing engineering[24] and undoubtedly provided a great climate for innovations. It is unfortunate that the records of the Manchester Literary and Philosophical Society were destroyed in the blitz of 1940,[25] for they might have yielded more insight into the above relationships. However, one does get a better picture of the excitement of the times that Church showed in his writings.

The most significant addition to Urwick's biography was Church's role with *The Engineering Magazine* as its European editor or manager from about 1903 to 1909. This makes Urwick's comment on when Church arrived in the United States probably a misinterpretation largely based on Urwick's 1906 attribution to Church from the *American Machinist*.[26] Church must have had a very good and a very strong and a very broad background at *The Engineering Magazine* and clearly this experience greatly benefited both his writing ability and his writing scope. It is unfortunate that his relationship with John R. Dunlap could not have been explored, as Dunlap probably deserved a spot in Urwick's list of pioneers of management. It certainly seems that there was quite a good fit between Dunlap and Church.

Church surely had a broad work experience. Once again, though, invaluable records of Church's efforts have been destroyed. It is also interesting to note that Church did not have long stays as an employee with C. H. Scovell & Company or with Patterson, Teele, & Dennis. Whether this was due to Church becoming more of a "loner" is an interesting supposition. Both these firms were very interested in factory costs and factory systems, so Church would have been in an environment similar to his work experience in England. Since Scovell was a strong proponent with Church of the imputation of interest, it would have been interesting to explore their relationship but no records remain of the once substantial firm of Scovell, Wellington and the records of Patterson, Teele & Dennis for 1913 are also almost non-existent.[27] This is also true for the Winchester Repeating Arms Company, one of the key companies in the United States in World War I and one in which Church and its president, John E. Otterson, may have had close contact.[28] The Winchester consulting assignment was not mentioned by Urwick[29] and would appear to have been a very significant one for Church. His experience with the Mount Hope Finishing Company was about 12 to 14 years and also no longer traceable.[30] There is, at least, a much fuller resume presented in terms of work experience than in Urwick.

Church published a great deal more than was noted by Urwick, *The Accountant's Index*, *The Engineering Index*, and *The Reader's Guide to Periodical Literature*. The most significant of these non-indexed writings are: (1) the 1912 comments on the Report on Administration of the ASME subcommittee; (2) the 1915 exchange with H. L. Gantt; (3) the 1915 articles on reports, (4) the 1922 articles on the Mount Hope Finishing experience; and (5) the 1934 attribution from the *Cost and Production Handbook*. The writer has thumbed through the pages of the *American Machinist* from 1912 through 1916, *Industrial Management* from 1916 through 1927, and *Factory and Industrial Management* from 1927 to 1933 and looked for writings by Church. This monograph does add a significant number of writings not previously listed and puts all the known writings in one list. Church was much more productive than one would imagine from reading Urwick.

Church's character has been inaccurately described at times too. If he were as shy as Urwick has made him to be,[31] this shyness came later than 1915. Church gave at least three public speeches: (1) in 1911 to the National Tool Builders Association; (2) in 1912 at the ASME subcommittee's discussion; and (3) in 1915 at the San Francisco International Engineering Congress. He certainly was not shy in using the rhetorical technique of a strawman. In addition, he certainly was an optimist, especially in the role of the United States as the place for manufacturing innovations. He certainly was a hard worker. For example, his 1914 book was "somewhat hurriedly written in the midst of professional work. ..."[32]

His most telling characteristic—covered fairly well by Urwick—was his humanity. Church was a very, very humane person. He wanted a square deal between workers and management. He believe that good habits could be taught. He was very considerate of the workers and the foremen. He believed in worker committee rather than paternalistic decisions. He did not want to get management involved in the worker's personal life. He was willing to give L. P. Alford much of the credit for their 1912 article. While Church was very concerned with machines, he was also very concerned with men.

Relationships of Church with the Early Pioneers of Management

It truly must have been an exciting time for those involved in the development of management in the last decades of the 1800's and the first two decade of the 1900's. It surely must also have been for Church, as he was involved with some of the most noted people of those years. Joseph Slater Lewis was his first mentor. Lewis mentioned Church in the preface of his 1895 book. Church and others made references to the relationship between him and Lewis. Hans Renold certainly was enamored by Church's system, although Hans Renold never made reference to Church. L. P. Alford and Church were not only collaborators in 1912 but maintained a close working relationship through 1934. One can conclude that Church was very well acquainted and a valued co-worker with 3 of the 70 people designated as the early pioneers of management by Urwick.

There was a second tier of involvement with three other pioneers. Carl Barth was critical of Church's comments at the discussion of the 1912 ASME subcommittee report and was associated with Church, or at least Church's consulting firm, at the Winchester Repeating Arms Company. Dexter S. Kimball was quite laudatory of Church's efforts. H. L. Gantt and Church had a somewhat vitrolic exchange of letters but seemed to have a mutual respect for each other. One can conclude that Church and his works were well known, if not totally accepted, by these three early pioneers.

A third tier of three of the early pioneers involved those whose works were reviewed by Church, mostly in a favorable light. They were Harrington Emerson, James Rowan, and Frederick Halsey. One can conclude that Church made at least some effort to be up-to-date in his readings.

His relationship with Frederick Winslow Taylor is discussed a little later in this chapter. Church was greatly influenced by the writings of Charles Babbage, who was concerned with topics such as machinery, general managerial principles, analysis of manufacturing processes and costs, time study, comparative management studies, and data processing. The writer is of the opinion that Church considered himself to be the Babbage of his era, although Church never specifically claimed this. What is needed is first to recognize the wisdom of Church, tie it into the works of Babbage, and then update these efforts for the end of this century and the beginning of the third millennium. There is someone out there as well versed as Church and Babbage in the fields of accounting, management, industrial engineering, and business and society. It is hoped that that someone will be inspired by this monograph to take on this crucial task.

An Holistic View of Church's Writings

There are many reasons why an holistic view of Church's writings had not occurred until this monograph. One of the reasons is that there are writings not listed in either *The Accountant's Index*, *The Engineering Index*, *Reader's Guide to Periodical Literature*, or Urwick. Another reason is that none of these four sources include more than about half his writings, so one has to consult all four to get a listing which is still only partial. Another reason is that the 1923 book was almost not reviewed at all, either at the time or later. Church's writings in business and society and in industrial engineering apparently have not been reviewed at all.

Church's 1910, 1914, 1917, 1929, and 1930 books were subjected to the standard review process, which excluded any significant comments on the author's prior efforts. Garner, Wells, Solomons, and Brummet did fine, but limited, jobs in reviewing Church's accounting works. Garner did not pull together his many references to Church and because of the 1925 cut-off date on his book, Garner did not review in detail Church's later efforts. Wells had a cut-off date of 1913 and, hence, missed much of Church's works in accounting. Solomons and Brummet did not give Church very extensive coverage. Jelinek and Litterer did fine jobs in reviewing Church's management writings, except for the 1923 book. However, Jelinek and Litterer made relatively token references to Church's accounting writings.

One can safely conclude, therefore, that no holistic review of Church's efforts had been made, even though he had a significant number of central themes in his writings in the four fields. This writer obviously hopes that this monograph is, at least, an acceptable holistic review.

Case Studies of Church's Systems
in Management Accounting

There probably is enough information in the archives of the Renold Company to piece together some interesting cases of Church's machine-hour-rate system. One's time could be well spent there, especially in light of writings by Church, Hans Renold, Sir Charles Renold, Roland Dunkerley, and the accounting reviewers just discussed. A close review of the Urwick and Wolf second edition of *The Golden Book of Management* gives plenty of examples of case studies, for which historical studies could be done. There are seven other case study topics from Church that have potential for today. They are: (1) group incentive systems and related accounting disclosures; (2) various methods of counters for measurement of key information; (3) time studies; (4) effects of various incentive systems on both manufacturing and non-manufacturing workers; (5) wastes and marketing of them; (6) changing wastes to scrap and scrap to by-products; and (7) effect on performance of long runs of repeat orders. Church's writings were certainly benefited by his "hands-on" experiences and could be used as models for write-ups of solutions "out there" now.

Engineering Input into Management
and Accounting

Church was considered by some to be an electrical engineer,[33] labeled himself as being an engineer before being an accountant,[34] and frequently classified himself as an industrial engineer. He clearly brought many engineering skills with him to his writings. Of the 11 pioneers mentioned as being somehow related to Church, all were engineers but Babbage[35] and Emerson[36]. Engineering input into accounting included many more writers than just Church.[37] It is doubtful that engineers today play anywhere near such a vital role in either management or accounting. After reviewing Church's work, and briefly looking at some of the work done by the engineering pioneers in management, this writer longs for much more engineering inputs now. The age of robotics requires the same degree of input from engineers into management and accounting as did the 1890's. Engineers should not only know and be proud of the early contributions by the pioneers to management and accounting but also should strive to emulate them.

Scientific Management
and Church

Jelinek's article somewhat prepared the writer for a seeming conflict between Taylor and Church[38]. However, the writer found the conflict really to have been almost an open war between Church and Alford on one side and the Taylorites, led by Barth and Gantt on the other. Not only did there appear, looking back 70 years, to be a substantial intellectual difference but there was open differences and warlike maneuvers in the decade of the 1910's.

There were at least seven instances of public blows by or on Church in the struggle with the Taylorites. The first blow was struck in the April, 1911 article on "The Meaning of Scientific Management," in the preface of which the editor of *The Engineering Magazine* put Church as a contemporary of Taylor and a predecessor of Gantt.[39] Church stressed his unique solutions theme in that article and introduced his two principles of management model.[40] In another 1911 article, he pointed out the differences between the Taylorites and him on the issue of the role of foremen in the new industrial world.[41] The third blow was the May 30, 1912 collaboration with L. P. Alford. They attacked Taylor directly in this article for his failure to develop principles of management.[42] The fourth blow was the skillful maneuvering by Alford to get the Church/Alford three principles model into the ASME sub-committee report.[43] While Church did not appear to strike a blow in his discussion of the report,[44] Barth thought so and gave a mild defense of Taylor's attention to the importance of machinery.[45] The fifth blow was thus a retaliation by the Taylorites.

The sixth blow was delivered by Church in his 1914 book. He switched the focus from Taylor and Emerson to their imitators.[46] He stressed the ASME adoption of the Church/Alford three principles.[47] The most exciting blow, or blows, was the exchange between Gantt and Church on the issue of overhead distribution. Church's first response to Gantt's article was relatively mild.[48] Gantt's was not, as he claimed Taylor had predated Church on the machine hour rate approach.[49] Gantt wrote "...I cannot imagine he really believes me to be as ignorant of the present methods of costing as he assumes I am..."[50] Church's second response was again mild,[51] as was Gantt's rejoiner.[52]

Perhaps Church was too vigorous in using the strawman of "Taylor imitators" and this might have been one of the reasons that hostility was present between Church and Taylor's supporters. Perhaps Church thought that an aggressive approach was necessary to obtain attention to his ideas. Perhaps he was appalled at the lack of concern for workers that the "Taylor imitators" showed. The writer believes all three reasons were present and that Church was somewhat guilty of again over-extending the rhetorical device of the strawman. It is quite probable that Church did lose any chance he had for a loyal following, or disciples, by being opposed to the well-established Taylor school. For every 1,000 people who recognize the name of Frederick Winslow Taylor there may be one in that group who would recognize Church's name. Church was undoubtedly right in his stressing of general principles over techniques but he has been relegated to oblivion. To the extent this oblivion was in retaliation for his attacks on the "Taylor imitators" is mere conjecture. Clearly, there was a war between Church and the supporters of Taylor.

Future Work

The first item for future work is the reading of selected, most, or all of Church's work. The reader will not be disappointed in his quest. The second item is an audit of *The Accountant's Index, 1920* for possible articles and books from engineering sources that are not listed. The third item is related and involves *The Engineering Index*. It should be updated for such exclusions as the *American Machinist* from 1912 to 1916 and have an author's index compiled for the years in which there were none.

The fourth item would be further work done on Church's background in England from family, education, and work points of study. The fifth item is a careful mining of the excellent archives at the Renold Company in Manchester, England. The sixth would be study of the use of the machine-hour rate method in practice and in texts from about 1910 to 1940, using the 1934 reference of *Cost and Production Handbook* section on that topic. The seventh entails a search of the writings and letters of the "Taylor imitators" to note further reactions to Church. The eighth is a study of the use of the imputation of interest by the Winchester Repeating Arms Company during World War I.

The ninth item is quite limitless and entails a following-up on the ideas of Church. Much can be gained from a pondering of each of the 125 ideas. Church was a man of action; he wrote about that what he saw and what could be done to improve what he saw. Remember that each solution is unique but that there are some general principles. If only five of the 125 ideas yield the reader some benefit, this monograph is a success.

FOOTNOTES

Footnotes for Chapter 2

[1] Urwick, Lyndall and Wolf, William B., *The Golden Book of Management: New Expanded Edition, in Two Parts* (New York: American Management Associations, 1984), p. 116.

[2] Colley. F. G.. "A Book Review of *The Science and Practices of Management*." *The Journal of Accountancy.* Dec., 1914. p. 484.

[3] Ibid.

[4] Urwick and Wolf, op. cit., p. 116.

[5] Ibid. [6] Ibid.,p. 57. [7] Ibid., p. 116.

[8] Letter of Mr. Keppel Massey to G. E. Royle, Commercial Manager, B. & S. Massey Ltd., about the writer's inquiry about Church, April 5, 1984.

[9] Ibid. [10] Ibid.

[11] Telephone Conversation with C. B. H. Gill, former partner in Parkinson, Mather & Co., in Manchester, England, on October, 1984.

[12] Manchester Society of Chartered Accountants, "A Brief History of the Manchester Society of Chartered Accountants," undated, p. 1.

[13] Urwick and Wolf, op. cit., p. 116.

[14] Cooley listed Church's arrival in the United States in 1909 and that he had been European Editor of *The Engineering Magazine* for 7 years. This places a maximum stay of 3 years at Renold.

[15] Urwick and Wolf, op. cit., p. 116.

[16] Ibid., pp. 116-7. [17] Ibid., p. 116.

[18] H., F. A., "Cost and Time-Keeping Outfit of the Taylor System: Some Conveniences and Short Cuts of Obvious Utility," *American Machinist*, December 13, 1906, pp. 761-3.

[19] Colley, op. cit., p. 484.

[20] Alford, L. P., Editor, *Management Engineering*, in his note to Church's "Internal Transportation in a Large Textile Finishing Plant," April, 1922, p. 197.

[21] Colley, op. cit., p. 484. [22] Ibid., pp. 484-5. [23] Ibid, p. 484.

[24] Diemer, Hugo, "A Bibliography of Works Management," *The Engineering Magazine*, July 2, 1904, pp. 626-42. "Index to the Periodical Literature of Industrial Engineering," *The Engineering Magazine*, July 2, 1904, pp. 643-58.

[25] Ibid.

[26] Editor, "Inspiring Growth of the New Science of Industrial Management," *Industrial Management: The Engineering Magazine*, November, 1916, p. 148.

[27] "Dunlap, John Robertson," *The National Cyclopaedia of American Biography*, Volume C, (New York: James T. White & Company, 1930), p. 434.

[28] "Inspiring Growth," op. cit., p. 148c.

[29] Wells, M. C., *Accounting for Common Costs*, (Champaign-Urbana, Center for International Education and Research in Accounting, 1978), p. 82 (footnote).

[30] Wells, M. C., *A Bibliography of Cost Accounting: Parts I and II*, Monograph 10, (Champaign-Urbana, Center for International Education and Research in Accounting, 1978), p. 442.

[31] Church, A. Hamilton, "Intensive Production and the Foreman," *American Machinist*, May 4, 1911, p. 830.

[32] Church, A. Hamilton, "Has 'Scientific Management' Science?", *American Machinist*, July 20, 1911, p. 108.

[33] The American Society of Mechanical Engineers (ASME), *Transactions: Volume 34, Cleveland Meeting New York Meeting, 1912* (New York: ASME, 1913), p. 1156.

[34] Church, A. Hamilton, "On the Inclusion of Interest in Manufacturing Costs," *The Journal of Accountancy*, April, 1913, p. 236.

[35] Urwick and Wolf, op. cit., p. 116.

[36] Personal correspondence with Lloyd A. Barnstead, who was a partner in Patterson, Teele & Dennis in New York, July 10, 1984.

[37] Church, A. Hamilton, "Industrial Management," Paper 238, *Transactions of The International Engineering Congress: San Francisco*, 1915, p. 446.

[38] Mee, John F., "Pater Familae et Magister," (Father of Family and Teacher), *Academy of Management Journal*, March, 1965, p. 17.

[39] Church, "Internal Transportation...," op. cit., p. 197. [40] Ibid.

[41] Urwick and Wolf, op. cit., p. 117.

[42] Letter from John Milliken, President of Mount Hope Finishing Company, to the writer in early 1983.

[43] Church, "Internal Transportation...," op. cit., p. 197.

[44] Church, A. Hamilton, "Selecting a Plant-Transport System: The Tractor-Skid-Ramp Method Applied to Textile Mills," *Industrial Management*, Dec., 1927, p. 368.

[45] Church, A. Hamilton, "Overhead—Cost of Production Preparedness," *Factory and Industrial Management*, January, 1931, p. 38.

[46] Alford, L. P., Editor, *Cost and Production Handbook*, (New York: The Ronald Press, 1934), iv.

[47] Church, "Selecting a Plant-Transport System," op. cit., p. 368.

[48] Conversation with Mr. Degan of the Degan Funeral Home on December 29, 1982.

[49] Letter from Thomas L. Crum, Rector of St. Thomas Episcopal Church in Taunton, Massachusetts, on December 31, 1982.

[50] Conversation with City Clerk in Taunton Massachusetts in 1984.

[51] Probate Court Records for the estate of Alexander Hamilton Church, Taunton, Massachusetts.

[52] Ibid.

[53] Review of *The Engineering Index*, 1913-6.

[54] Review of *The Engineering Index*.

[55] Lewis, J. Slater, *The Commercial Organization of Factories: A Handbook for the Use of Manufacturers, Directors, Auditors, Engineers, Managers, Secretaries, Accountants, Cashiers, Estimate Clerks, Prime Cost Clerks, Bookkeepers, Draughtsmen, Students, Pupils, etc.* (London: E. & R. N. Spon, 1896), vii.

[56] Ibid.

[57] Urwick and Wolf, op. cit., p. 55.

[58] Lewis, op. cit., vii.

[59] Urwick and Wolf, op. cit., p. 57.

[60] Lewis, J. Slater, "Works Management for Maximum Production," *The Engineering Magazine*, May, 1900, p. 211.

[61] Ibid.

[62] Church, A. Hamilton, "The Meaning of Commercial Organization," *The Engineering Magazine*, December, 1900, p. 391.

[63] Editors of *The Engineering Magazine*, in a note preceding Church's "The Meaning of Scientific Management," *The Engineering Magazine*, April, 1911, p. 97.

[64] Urwick and Wolf, op. cit., p. 58. [65] Ibid., p. 59.

[66] Renold, Hans, "Engineering Workshop Organization," *Proceedings, Manchester Association of Engineers*, Discussion Session, 1913-14, p. 27.

[67] "Obituary: Percy O. Lightbody," *Management Accounting*, (UK) January, 1965, p. 34.

[68] Ibid.

[69] "First Award of the Institute Gold Medal: Presentation to Mr. Roland Dunkerley, JP, FCWA," *The Cost Accountant*, July, 1955, p. 62.

[70] Dunkerley, Roland, "A Historical Review of the Institute and the Profession," *The Cost Accountant*, September-November, 1946, p. 17.

[71] Urwick and Wolf, op. cit., p. 184.

[72] Ibid., p. 186.

[73] Alford, op. cit., title page.

[74] ASME, *Transactions: Volume 34*, op. cit., p. 1147.

[75] Merrill, Harwood F. Editor, *Classics in Management* (New York: American Management Association, 1960, p. 197.

[76] Ibid., p. 196.

[77] Urwick and Wolf, op. cit., p. 86.

[78] ASME, *Transactions: Volume 34*, op. cit., p. 1204.

[79] Mee, op. cit., p. 17. [80] Ibid.

[81] Urwick and Wolf, op. cit., p. 106.

[82] Kimball, Dexter S., "Review of Manufacturing Costs and Accountants," *American Machinist*, March 8, 1917, p. 396.

[83] Urwick and Wolf, op. cit., pp. 95-6.

[84] See Chapter 4, 1915 section.

[85] Urwick and Wolf, op. cit., pp. 62. [86] Ibid., p. 61.

[87] Church, A. Hamilton. *The Proper Distribution of Expense Burden*, Works Management Library (London: The Engineering Magazine, 1908), pp. 9-10.

[88] Church, A. Hamilton, "Bonus Systems and the Expense Burden," *The Engineering Magazine*, November, 1913, p. 207.

[89] Urwick and Wolf, op. cit., pp. 24-5. [90] Ibid., p. 79.

[91] Jaffe, William J., *L. P. Alford and The Evolution of Modern Industrial Management* (New York: New York University Press, 1957), pp. 137-8.

[92] Urwick and Wolf, op. cit., p. 81. [93] Ibid., pp. 81-2.

[94] ASME, *Transactions: Volume 34*, op. cit., pp. 1156-9 and pp. 1194-1201.

[95] Urwick and Wolf, op. cit., p. 50. [96] Ibid., p. 76. [97] Ibid., p. 115.

[98] Ibid. [99] Ibid.

[100] Church, A. Hamilton, "Distribution of the Expense Burden," *American Machinist*, May 25, 1911, p. 991, p. 999.

[101] ASME, *Transactions Volume 34*, op. cit., pp. 1153-1226.

[102] Church, "Industrial Management," op. cit., p. 446.

[103] Ibid., p. 472.

Footnotes for Chapter 3

[1] Church, *The Proper Distribution*, op. cit., pp. 14-5.

[2] Ibid., pp. 22-3. [3] Ibid., p. 24. [4] Ibid. [5] Ibid., pp. 28-9.

[6] Ibid., p. 40. [7] Ibid., p. 41. [8] Ibid., p. 43. [9] Ibid., pp. 44-5

[10] Ibid., pp. 53-4. [11] Ibid., p. 57. [12] Ibid., p. 85. [13] Ibid., pp. 94-5.

[14] Ibid., p. 99. [15] Ibid., p. 101. [16] Ibid., p. 102. [17] Ibid., pp. 114-5.

[18] Garner, S. Paul, *Evolution of Cost Accounting to 1925*, Accounting History Classics Series, original edition, 1954, reprint edition, 1976 (University, Alabama: The University of Alabama Press, 1976), Index.

[19] Ibid., Editor's forward. [20] Ibid., p. 134. [21] Ibid., p. 187. [22] Ibid., p. 225. [23] Ibid., p. 191.

[24] Wells, *A Bibliography of Cost Accounting*, op. cit.

[25] Wells, *Accounting for Common Costs*, op. cit.

[26] Ibid., pp. 79-91. [27] Ibid., p. 80. [28] Ibid., p. 81.

[29] Ibid. [30] Ibid., p. 82. [31] Ibid., p. 87.

[32] Wells, *A Bibliography of Costs*, op. cit., p. 419 and p. 235.

[33] Ibid., p. 241. [34] Ibid., p. 441. [35] Ibid., p. 871.

[36] Solomons, David, "The Historical Development of Costing," in *Studies in Cost Analysis*, edited by himself, 2nd Edition (Homewood, Illinois: Richard D. Irwin, Inc., 1968), pp. 24-8.

[37] Ibid., p. 26. [38] Ibid., p. 28. [39] Ibid., p. 27.

[40] Renold, Sir Charles, "Management Accounts," *The Cost Accountant*, September, 1950, pp. 108-28.

[41] Ibid., p. 113. [42] Ibid. [43] Ibid.

[44] Ibid. [45] Ibid., p. 113, p. 116. [46] Ibid., p. 116.

[47] Brummet, R. Lee, *Overhead Costing: The Costing of Manufactured Products* (Ann Arbor: Bureau of Business Research, 1957).

[48] Ibid., p. 12. [49] Ibid. [50] Ibid., p. 7. [51] Ibid. [52] Ibid., pp. 9-11.

[53] Litterer, Joseph A., "Alexander Hamilton Church and the Development of Modern Management," *Business History Review*, Winter, 1961, p. 224.

[54] Solomons, op. cit., p. 26.

[55] Church, *The Proper Distribution*, op. cit., pp. 14-5.

[56] Ibid., p. 23.

[57] Church, A. Hamilton, *Production Factors in Cost Accounting and Works Management*, Industrial Management Library (New York: The Engineering Magazine, 1919), p. 10.

[58] Ibid., p. 23. [59] Ibid., pp. 22-3. [60] Ibid., p. 38. [61] Ibid., p. 61. [62] Ibid., p. 45.

[63] Ibid., pp. 47-8, p. 54. [64] Ibid., p. 122. [65] Ibid., p. 124. [66] Ibid., p. 125.

[67] Ibid., p. 126. [68] Ibid., p. 127. [69] Ibid., p. 128. [70] Ibid., pp. 149-50.

[71] Ibid., pp. 152-3. [72] Ibid., p. 153. [73] Ibid., pp. 158-9. [74] Ibid., p. 162. [75] Ibid., pp. 169-70.

[76] Ibid., p. 170. [77] Ibid., pp. 172-3. [78] Ibid., p. 171. [79] Ibid., p. 176.

[80] Ibid., p. 182. [81] Garner, op. cit., p. 184. [82] Ibid., p. 226. [83] Ibid., p. 137.

[84] Wells, *Accounting for Common Costs*, op. cit., pp. 82-6.

[85] Ibid., p. 87.

[86] Wells, *A Bibliography of Cost Accounting*, op. cit., p. 844.

[87] Ibid., p. 262. [88] Ibid., p. 457. [89] Ibid., p. 277. [90] Ibid., p. 520. [91] Ibid., p. 926.

[92] Galloway, Lee, "Review of *Production Factors in Cost Accounting and Works Management*," *The Journal of Accountancy*, May, 1911, p. 74.

[93] Ibid.

[94] Church, *The Proper Distribution*, op. cit., p. 22.

[95] Church, "Distribution of the Expense Burden," op. cit., pp. 991-2, 999.

[96] Church, A. Hamilton, "Distributing Expense Burden: The Analysis Based Upon the Capacity to Produce, Net Upon the Cost of Production," *The Iron Age*, pp. 1325-6.

[97] Church, "Distribution of the Expense Burden," op. cit., p. 991.

[98] Ibid. [99] Ibid. [100] Ibid. [101] Ibid. [102] Ibid., p. 992. [103] Ibid., p. 999. [104] Ibid.

[105] Church, A. Hamilton, "Direct and Indirect Costs," Letters to the Editor Section, *American Machinist*, May 9, 1912, p. 763.

[106] Ibid. [107] Ibid. [108] Ibid. [109] Ibid.

[110] "The Treatment of Interest on Manufacturing Investment," *The Journal of Accountancy*, April, 1913, pp. 231-44.

[111] Ibid., p. 231.

[112] Cole, William Morse, "The Interest on Investment in Equipment," *The Journal of Accountancy*, April, 1913, p. 236.

[113] Church, "On the Inclusion of Interest...," op. cit., pp. 236-7.

[114] Ibid., p. 237. [115] Ibid., p. 240. [116] Ibid.

[117] Richards, W. G., "Interest Not a Charge Against Costs," *The Journal of Accountancy*, April, 1913, pp. 240-1.

[118] Sterrett, J. E., "Interest Not a Part of the Cost of Production," *The Journal of Accountancy*, April, 1913, pp. 241-4.

[119] Mee, op. cit., p. 17.

[120] Williamson, Harold F., *Winchester: The Gun that Won the West*, (Washington, D.C.: Combat Forces Press, 1952), p. 240.

[121] Ibid. [122] Ibid., p. 407.

[123] Jelinek, Mariann, "Toward Systematic Management: Alexander Hamilton Church," *Business History Review*, Spring, 1980, pp. 75-6.

[124] Ibid., p. 75 and p. 76.

[125] Brummet, op. cit., p. 4.

Footnotes for Chapter 4

1 The writer was told that statement a number of years ago by the Head Librarian of the AICPA. This is substantiated by a comment in *The Accountants Index: 1921-23*, which discusses borrowing privileges of members of material in the Library in the Introductory Note from Louise S. Miltimore, Librarian.

2 A search of both the entries for Gantt and Church in *The Accountant's Index* failed to note these articles.

3 Gantt, H. L., "The Relation Between Production and Costs," *American Machinist*, June 17, 1915, p. 1055.

4 Ibid. 5 Ibid., p. 1056. 6 Ibid. 7 Ibid. 8 Ibid., p. 1062.

9 Church, A. Hamilton, "Mr. Gantt's Theory of the Expense Burden," in the Discussion of Previous Question section, *American Machinist*, July 29, 1915, p. 209.

10 Ibid., p. 210. 11 Ibid. 12 Ibid. 13 Ibid.

14 Gantt, H. L., "Relation Between Production and Cost," in the Discussion of Previous Question section, *American Machinist*, August 26, 1915, pp. 385-6.

15 Ibid., p. 385. 16 Ibid., p. 386. 17 Ibid.

18 Church, A. Hamilton, "Relation Between Cost and Production," in the Discussion of Previous Question section, *American Machinist*, September 2, 1915, p. 431.

19 Ibid.

20 Gantt, H. L., "Relation Between Production and Cost," in the Discussion of Previous Question section, *American Machinist*, October 21, 1915, p. 737.

21 Ibid. 22 Ibid.

23 McHenry, William E. M., "Relation Between Production and Cost," in the Discussion of Previous Question section, *American Machinist*, September 23, 1915, p. 564.

24 Ibid. 25 Ibid.

26 Church, A. Hamilton, *Manufacturing Costs and Accounts* (New York: McGraw-Hill Book Company, Inc., 1917)

27 Church, A. Hamilton, *Manufacturing Costs and Accounts* (New York: McGraw Hill Book Company, Inc., 1929)

28 Church, *Manufacturing Costs and Accounts*, 1st Edition, op. cit., v.

29 Ibid., pp. 12-36. 30 Ibid., p. 79. 31 Ibid., pp. 87-8. 32 Ibid., p. 257.

33 Ibid., p. 340. 34 Ibid., p. 353. 35 Ibid., p. 356. 36 Ibid., pp. 393-4.

37 Church, *Manufacturing Costs and Accounts*, 2nd Edition, op. cit., v.

38 Ibid., pp. 302-3. 39 Ibid., insert between p. 410 and p. 411.

40 Garner, op. cit., p. 172.

41 Ibid., p. 297. 42 Ibid., p. 304. 43 Ibid. 44 Ibid., p. 240. 45 Ibid., pp. 155-7.

46 See footnote 31 for Chapter 2.

47 Garner, op. cit., p. 156.

48 Kimball, op. cit., p. 396.

49 Ibid. 50 Ibid. 51 Ibid. 52 Ibid. 53 Ibid.

54 Cameron, A. T., "Review of *Manufacturing Costs and Accounts*," *Annals of the American Academy of Political and Social Science*, November, 1917, p. 294.

55 Ibid.

56 Greeley, Harold Dudley, "Review of *Manufacturing Costs and Accounts*," *The Journal of Accountancy*, June, 1917, p. 477

57 Ibid., p. 475. 58 Ibid., p. 476. 59 Ibid.

60 Going, Charles Buxton, "Review of *Manufacturing Costs and Accounts*," *The Journal of American Society of Mechanical Engineers*, April, 1917, pp. 369-70.

61 Ibid., p. 369. 62 Ibid. 63 Ibid., p. 370. 64 Ibid.

65 Going, Charles Buxton, "The Efficiency Movement. An Outline," *Transactions of the Efficiency Society*, Vol. 1 No. 1, 1912, p. 11.

66 Potter, R. R., "Review of *Manufacturing Costs and Accounts*," *Engineering News-Record*, April 19, 1917, p. 150

67 Coffman, Paul B., "Review of *Manufacturing Costs and Accounts*," *The Accounting Review*, April, 1930, pp. 86-7

68 van Oss, A., "Review of *Manufacturing Costs and Accounts*," *The Journal of Accountancy*, July, 1929, p. 73.

69 Ibid.

[70] Church, A. Hamilton, *Overhead Expense: In Relation to Costs, Sales and Profits* (New York: McGraw-Hill Book Company, Inc., 1930).

[71] Church, "Overhead Costs....," op.cit., pp. 38-41.

[72] Church, *Overhead Expense*, op. cit., v.

[73] Ibid., vi. [74] Ibid., v. [75] Ibid., p. 1. [76] Ibid., p. 3. [77] Ibid., p. 5.

[78] Ibid., p. 7. [79] Ibid., p. 7. [80] Ibid., p. 9. [81] Ibid., p. 11. [82] Ibid., p. 14. [83] Ibid., p. 15.

[84] Ibid., p. 16. [85] Ibid., p. 21. [86] Ibid., pp. 22-7. [87] Ibid., pp. 43-54. [88] Ibid., p. 51.

[89] Ibid., p. 55. [90] Ibid., p. 66. [91] Ibid., pp. 82-3. [92] Ibid., p. 84. [93] Ibid.

[94] Ibid., p. 87. [95] Ibid. [96] Ibid., p. 90. [97] Ibid., p. 109. [98] Ibid.

[99] Ibid., p. 118. [100] Ibid., p. 119. [101] Ibid., p. 122. [102] Ibid., p. 124. [103] Ibid., p. 127.

[104] Ibid., p. 129. [105] Ibid., p. 156. [106] Ibid., p. 178. [107] Ibid., pp. 383-4.

[108] Ibid., p. 158. [109] Ibid., pp. 194-5. [110] Ibid., p. 257. [111] Ibid., p. 216.

[112] Ibid., p. 220. [113] Ibid., p. 253. [114] Ibid., p. 265. [115] Ibid., p. 275.

[116] Ibid., p. 284-5. [117] Ibid., p. 283. [118] Ibid., p. 307. [119] Ibid., p. 305. [120] Ibid., p. 337.

[121] Ibid., pp. 395-6. [122] Ibid., pp. 410-1.

[123] Church, "Overhead Costs....," op. cit., pp. 38-41.

[124] Ibid., p. 38. [125] Ibid. [126] Ibid. [127] Ibid., p. 39. [128] Ibid., p. 41. [129] Ibid.

[130] Garner, op. cit., p. 243.

[131] Brummet, op. cit., p. 10.

[132] Coffman, P. B., "Review of Overhead Expenses," *The Accounting Review*, March, 1931, p. 82.

[133] Thornton, Frank W., "Review of Overhead Expense," *The Journal of Accountancy*, August, 1930, p. 150.

[134] Ibid.

[135] See Footnote 73 for Chapter 2.

[136] Alford, L. P., Editor, *Cost and Production Handbook*, op. cit., p. 1085.

[137] Ibid.

[138] Ibid. [139] Ibid. [140] Ibid., pp. 1085-7. [141] Ibid., p. 242-5. [142] Ibid., p. 243.

Footnotes for Chapter 5

[1] See footnote 61 in Chapter 2.

[2] See footnote 59 in Chapter 2.

[3] Church, A. Hamilton, "The Meaning of Commercial Organization," *The Engineering Magazine*, December, 1900, p. 391.

[4] Ibid. [5] Ibid. [6] Ibid., p. 392. [7] Ibid., p. 393. [8] Ibid., p. 394. [9] Ibid.

[10] Ibid., p. 395. [11] Ibid., p. 396. [12] Ibid., p. 394. [13] Ibid., p. 396. [14] Ibid., p. 397. [15] Ibid. [16] Ibid., p. 398.

[17] Litterer, op. cit., p. 212. [18] Ibid., p. 213.

[19] Jelinek, op.cit., p. 71. [20] Ibid., p. 72.

[21] Church, "The Meaning of Scientific Management," op. cit., pp. 97-101.

[22] See footnote 63 in Chapter 2.

[23] Church, "The Meaning of Scientific Management," op. cit., p. 97.

[24] Ibid., p. 98. [25] Ibid., p. 99. [26] Ibid., p. 100.

[27] Ibid., p. 100. [28] Ibid. [29] Ibid., p. 101. [30] Ibid.

[31] Church, A. Hamilton, "Intensive Production and the Foreman," *American Machinist*, May 4, 1911, pp. 830-1.

[32] Ibid., p. 830. [33] Ibid. [34] Ibid. [35] Ibid., pp. 830-1. [36] Ibid., p. 831. [37] Ibid.

[38] Merrill, op. cit., reprinting Church and Alford's, "The Principles of Management," p. 198.

[39] Ibid., p. 199. [40] Ibid. [41] Ibid., pp. 201-6. [42] Ibid., p. 206. [43] Ibid., pp. 206-9.

[44] Ibid., p. 209. [45] Ibid., p. 203. [46] Ibid., p. 203. [47] Ibid., p. 211.

[48] Ibid., p. 212. [49] Ibid., p. 213. [50] Ibid., p. 214.

[51] See footnote 76 in Chapter 2.

[52] ASME, *Transactions; Vol. 34*, op. cit., p. 1131.

[53] "Management," *American Machinist*, December 19, 1912, p. 1043.

[54] ASME, *Transactions: Vol. 34*, op. cit., p. 1142.

[55] Ibid., pp. 1153-1227. "Management," *American Machinist*, op. cit., p. 1043.

[56] ASME, *Transactions: Vol. 34*, op. cit., p. 1157.

[57] Ibid. [58] Ibid., p. 1158.

[59] Ibid. [60] Ibid., pp. 1158-9. [61] Ibid., p. 1204.

[62] Kimball, Dexter S., "The 'Principles of Management,'" *American Machinist*, June 13, 1912, p. 965.

[63] Ibid. [64] Ibid.

[65] Calder, J., "The Principles of Management," *American Machinist*, June 13, 1912, p. 965.

[66] Ibid.

[67] Merrill, op. cit., pp. 197-214.

[68] Ibid., p. 197. [69] Ibid. [70] Ibid.

[71] Wren, Daniel A., *The Evolution of Management Thought* (New York: The Ronald Press Company, 1972), pp. 183-4 and pp. 191-2.

[72] Ibid., pp. 183-4.

[73] Litterer, op. cit., p. 221.

[74] Jelinek, op. cit., p. 77.

[75] Alford, L. P. *Laws of Management: Applied to Manufacturing*, (New York: The Ronald Press Company, 1928.)

[76] Church, A. Hamilton, *The Science and Practice of Management*, Works Management Library (New York: The Engineering Magazine, 1914), v-vi.

[77] Ibid.

[78] Church, A. Hamilton, "The Scientific Basis of Manufacturing Manaement," and "What are the Principles of Management," *The Efficiency Journal*, February, 1914, pp. 8-15 and pp. 16-8.

[79] Church, *The Science and Practice of Management*, op. cit., iii-iv.

[80] Ibid., iv. [81] Ibid. [82] Ibid., p. 1. [83] Ibid., p. 2. [84] Ibid. [85] Ibid., pp. 3-4.

[86] Ibid., p. 4. [87] Ibid., p. 5. [88] Ibid., p. 10. [89] Ibid., p. 11. [90] Ibid., p. 17.

[91] Ibid., p. 21. [92] Ibid., pp. 22-3. [93] Ibid., p. 29. [94] Ibid., p. 35.

[95] Ibid., pp. 37-8. [96] Ibid., p. 44. [97] Ibid., p. 48. [98] Ibid., p. 53. [99] Ibid., pp. 54-5.

[100] Ibid., p. 63. [101] Ibid., p. 65. [102] Ibid. [103] Ibid., p. 70. [104] Ibid., p. 71. [105] Ibid., p. 74.

[106] Ibid., p. 75. [107] Ibid., p. 80. [108] Ibid. [109] Ibid., pp. 82-3. [110] Ibid., pp. 84-5.

[111] Ibid., p. 96. [112] Ibid., p. 99. [113] Ibid., p. 106. [114] Ibid., p. 111. [115] Ibid., p. 131.

[116] Ibid., p. 139. [117] Ibid., p. 151. [118] Ibid., p. 374. [119] Ibid., p. 175. [120] Ibid., p. 186.

[121] Ibid., p. 187. [122] Ibid., p. 208. [123] Ibid., pp. 216-7. [124] Ibid., pp. 232-3. [125] Ibid., p. 293.

[126] Ibid., pp. 241-2. [127] Ibid., p. 270. [128] Ibid., p. 400. [129] Ibid., p. 416. [130] Ibid., p. 432.

[131] Ibid., pp. 303-4. [132] Ibid., p. 321. [133] Ibid., p. 338. [134] Ibid., p. 348. [135] Ibid., p. 353.

[136] Jelinek, op. cit., p. 71. [137] Ibid. [138] Ibid. [139] Ibid., p. 73. [140] Ibid., p. 78.

[141] Litterer, op. cit., p. 214.

[142] Ibid. [143] Ibid., p. 220. [144] Ibid., p. 225. [145] Ibid.

[146] Wren, op. cit., p. 191. [147] Ibid., p. 192.

[148] See footnote 2 in Chapter 2.

[149] Colley, op. cit., p. 484.

[150] Ibid., p. 485. [151] Ibid., p. 486.

[152] Davis, Ralph Currier, *The Fundamentals of Top Management* (New York: Harper & Brothers, Publishers, 1951).

[153] Ibid., p. 23. [154] Ibid., p. 43. [155] Ibid., p. 205. [156] Ibid., p. 217. [157] Ibid., p. 635.

[158] Ibid., p. 718. [159] Mee, op. cit., p. 642. [160] Ibid., p. 643.

[161] Urwick and Wolf, op. cit., p. 115.

[162] Church, "Industrial Management," op. cit., pp. 446-72.

[163] Church, A. Hamilton, "What is a Cost System?," Sept. 9, 1915; "What a Foreman Should Know About Costs," Sept. 23. 1915; "What the Superintendent Should Know," Oct. 14, 1915; "What the Executive Wants to Know About Costs," Oct. 28, 1915; *American Machinist*; pp. 455-7; pp. 553-6; pp. 675-8; pp. 763-6, respectively.

[164] Church, *Manufacturing Cost and Accounts*, 1917, op. cit., p. 395 and pp. 397-447.

[165] Review of *The Engineering Index* for 1913-6.

[166] Review of *The Accountant's Index*, 1920.

[167] Church, "Industrial Management," op. cit., pp. 446-71.

[168] Ibid., p. 471.

[169] Church, "What is a Cost System," op. cit, pp. 455-7.

[170] Ibid., p. 455. [171] Ibid. [172] Ibid. [173] Ibid. [174] Ibid. [175] Ibid. [176] Ibid. [177] Ibid., p. 456.

[178] Ibid. [179] Ibid. [180] Ibid. [181] Ibid., p. 457. [182] Ibid. [183] Ibid.

[184] Church, "What a Foreman Should Know about Costs," op. cit., p. 553.

[185] Ibid., p. 555. [186] Ibid. [187] Ibid., p. 554. [188] Ibid. p. 555.

[189] Church, "What the Superintendent Should Know," op. cit., pp. 675-8.

[190] Ibid., p. 675. [191] Ibid., pp. 676-8.

[192] Church, "What the Executive Wants to Know about Costs," op. cit., pp. 763-6.

[193] Ibid., p. 763. [194] Ibid., pp. 763-6. [195] Ibid., p. 764.

[196] Morrison, C. J., "What a Foreman Should Know about Costs," in the Discussion of Previous Question section, *American Machinist*, Oct. 28, 1915, p. 782.

[197] Ibid.

[198] Jenckes, J. M. "What a Foreman Should Know about Costs," in the Discussion of Previous Question section, *American Machinist*, Nov. 11, 1915, p. 869.

[199] *The National Union Catalog: Pre—1956 Imprints*, (London: Mansell, 1970), Vol. 108, pp. 678-9.

[200] Church, A. Hamilton, *The Making of an Executive* (New York: D. Appleton & Co., 1923) from the Hive Management History Series: No. 3 (Easton: Hive Publishing Company, 1972), foreword.

[201] Ibid. [202] Ibid., p. 1. [203] Ibid., p. 2. [204] Ibid., p. 4. [205] Ibid., pp. 4-5. [206] Ibid., p. 7. [207] Ibid., p. 8.

[208] Ibid., p. 9. [209] Ibid. [210] Ibid., p. 10. [211] Ibid., p. 14. [212] Ibid., p. 18. [213] Ibid., p. 21. [214] Ibid., p. 22.

[215] Ibid. [216] Ibid. [217] Ibid., p. 28. [218] Ibid., pp. 31-47. [219] Ibid., pp. 548-52. [220] Ibid., pp. 52-5.

[221] Ibid., pp. 55-8. [222] Ibid., pp. 58-76. [223] Ibid., p. 60. [224] Ibid., pp. 60-1. [225] Ibid., p. 65, p. 76.

[226] Ibid., p. 78-131. [227] Ibid., p. 87. [228] Ibid., pp. 97-106. [229] Ibid., p. 124. [230] Ibid. p. 106. [231] Ibid., pp. 132-87.

[232] Ibid., p. 135. [233] Ibid., pp. 139-40. [234] Ibid., p. 150. [235] Ibid., pp. 188-237. [236] Ibid., p. 208.

[237] Ibid., p. 209. [238] Ibid., p. 234. [239] Ibid., pp. 238-86. [240] Ibid., pp. 238-9. [241] Ibid., p. 241. [242] Ibid., pp. 243-4.

[243] Ibid., p. 251. [244] Ibid., p. 259. [245] Ibid., p. 270. [246] Ibid., pp. 270-1. [247] Ibid., p. 274. [248] Ibid., p. 278.

[249] Ibid., p. 282. [250] Ibid., pp. 287-324. [251] Ibid., p. 287. [252] Ibid., p. 288. [253] Ibid., p. 291. [254] Ibid., p. 292.

[255] Ibid., p. 292-3. [256] Ibid., p. 293. [257] Ibid., p. 297. [258] Ibid., p. 305. [259] Ibid., p. 307.

[260] Ibid., pp. 325-63. [261] Ibid., pp. 346-7. [262] Ibid., pp. 364-409. [263] Ibid., p. 366. [264] Ibid., p. 367.

[265] Ibid., pp. 372. [266] Ibid., pp. 374-5. [267] Ibid., p. 376. [268] Ibid., p. 384. [269] Ibid., p. 392. [270] Ibid., p. 394.

[271] Ibid., p. 396. [272] Ibid., pp. 410-45. [273] Ibid., p. 412. [274] Ibid., p. 414. [275] Ibid., pp. 415. [276] Ibid., p. 418.

[277] Ibid., p. 421.

[278] See footnote 98 in Chapter 2.

[279] Garner, op. cit., p. 142 and p. 366.

Footnotes to Chapter 6

[1] Church, A. Hamilton, "British Industrial Welfare: The Erring Policy of the British Workingman," *Cassier's Magazine*, New York and London, March, 1901, pp. 404-8.

[2] Ferguson, Eugene S., *Bibliography of the History of Technology* (Cambridge, Mass: Society for the History of Technology, 1968), p. 157.

[3] Church, "British Industrial Welfare," op. cit., p. 404.

[4] Ibid. [5] Ibid., p. 405. [6] Ibid. [7] Ibid.

[8] Ibid., p. 406. [9] Ibid. [10] Ibid. [11] Ibid., p. 407. [12] Ibid.

[13] Review of introductory page of the April-June, 1917 issue of *The Unpopular Review* and an analysis of articles in the 1917 volume.

[14] Church, A. Hamilton, "The Future of Industry," *The Unpopular Review*, April-June, 1917, p. 252.

¹⁵ Ibid., p. 253. ¹⁶ Ibid., p. 254. ¹⁷ Ibid., p. 255. ¹⁸ Ibid., p. 258. ¹⁹ Ibid., pp. 258-9.

²⁰ Ibid., p. 262. ²¹ Ibid., p. 265. ²² Ibid., pp. 265-6. ²³ Ibid., p. 268. ²⁴ Ibid. ²⁵ Ibid., p. 272.

²⁶ Church, A. Hamilton, "Premium, Piecework, and the Expense Burden," *The Engineering Magazine*, October, 1913, pp. 7-18.

²⁷ Church, A. Hamilton, "Bonus Systems and the Expense Burden," *The Engineering Magazine*, November, 1913, pp. 207-16.

²⁸ Church, "Premium, Piecework, and the Expense Burden, op. cit., p. 7.

²⁹ Ibid. ³⁰ Ibid. ³¹ Ibid., p. 8. ³² Ibid. ³³ Ibid. ³⁴ Ibid. ³⁵ Ibid., p. 9. ³⁶ Ibid., pp. 12-3.

³⁷ Ibid., pp. 12-3, 15-6. ³⁸ Ibid., p. 11. ³⁹ Ibid., p. 14. ⁴⁰ Ibid. ⁴¹ Ibid., p. 11. ⁴² Ibid., p. 14. ⁴³ Ibid., p. 18.

⁴⁴ Church, "Bonus Systems and the Expense Burden," op. cit., p. 207.

⁴⁵ Ibid. ⁴⁶ Ibid., p. 208. ⁴⁷ Ibid., pp. 208-9. ⁴⁸ Ibid., p. 212. ⁴⁹ Ibid. ⁵⁰ Ibid.

⁵¹ Ibid., p. 213. ⁵² Ibid. ⁵³ Ibid., p. 214.

⁵⁴ Church, A. Hamilton, "The Evolution of Design," in the Discussion of Previous Question section, *American Machinist*, June 20, 1915, p. 1008.

⁵⁵ Ibid. ⁵⁶ Ibid. ⁵⁷ Ibid.

⁵⁸ Church, A. Hamilton, "Machine Design and the Design of Systems," *American Machinist*, July 8, 1915, p. 61.

⁵⁹ Ibid. ⁶⁰ Ibid. ⁶¹ Ibid. ⁶² Ibid., p. 62. ⁶³ Ibid. ⁶⁴ Ibid.

⁶⁵ Church, "Internal Transportation in a Large Textile Finishing Plant—I," op. cit., pp. 197-202 and "II", May, 1922, *Management Engineering*, pp. 293-6.

⁶⁶ Church, "Internal Transportation...I," op. cit., p. 202.

⁶⁷ Church, "Internal Transportation...II," op. cit., p. 293.

⁶⁸ Ibid.

⁶⁹ Church, A. Hamilton, "Selecting a Plant-Transport System...," op. cit., pp 368-71.

⁷⁰ Ibid., p. 368. ⁷¹ Ibid., p. 369. ⁷² Ibid. ⁷³ Ibid. ⁷⁴ Ibid. ⁷⁵ Ibid., p. 371.

Footnotes for Chapter 7

¹ Garner, op. cit., p. 191.

² Ibid., p. 172.

³ Kimball, op. cit., p. 396.

⁴ Cameron, op. cit., p. 294.

⁵ Greely, op. cit., p. 476.

⁶ Church, *The Proper Distribution of the Expense Burden*, op. cit., p. 14-5.

⁷ Ibid., p. 23.

⁸ Church, *Production Factors...*, op. cit, p. 22.

⁹ Church, *Manufacturing Costs and Accounts*, 1917, op. cit., preface.

¹⁰ Church, *The Making of an Executive*, op. cit, p. 348.

¹¹ Coffman, op. cit, p. 73.

¹² Church, *The Making of an Executive*, op. cit, p. 367.

¹³ Renold, op. cit., p. 113.

¹⁴ Dunkerley, op. cit., p. 17.

¹⁵ Galloway, op. cit, p. 74.

¹⁶ Church, *The Proper Distribution of the Expense Burden*, op. cit., p. 114-5.

¹⁷ Church, *Production Factors*, p. 172.

¹⁸ Church, *Manufacturing Costs and Accounts*, 1917, preface.

¹⁹ Church, *The Science and Practice of Management*, op. cit, p. 348.

²⁰ Colley, op. cit., p. 484.

²¹ Urwick and Wolf, op. cit., p. 116. Letter from Senator Claiborne Pell, RI, about research done on this topic by the Library of Congress staff.

²² Colley, op. cit., p. 484.

²³ Urwick and Wolf, op. cit., p. 116.

24 Makepiece, Chris E., *Science and Technology in Manchester: Two Hundred Years of the Lit. and Phil.* (Manchester: Manchester Literary & Philosophical Publications Ltd., 1984), pp. 44-52.

25 Ibid., p. 18.

26 Urwick and Wolf, op. cit., p. 116.

27 Letter to the writer from Mr. Roger Wellington, former partner in Scovell, Wellington and Letter to the writer from Mr. Lloyd Barnstead, former partner in Patterson, Teele, & Dennis.

28 Mee, op. cit., p. 17. Williamson, op. cit., p. 240. Phone calls to Winchester's parent company yielded no help as to the whereabouts of any of Winchester's past records.

29 Urwick and Wolf, op. cit., p. 117.

30 Letter from the current president of Mount Hope Finishing, Mr. John Milliken.

31 Urwick and Wolf, op. cit., p. 115.

32 Church, *The Science and Practice of Management*, op. cit., preface.

33 Urwick and Wolf, p.116.

34 Church, "Relation Between Production and Cost," Sept. 2, 1915, op. cit., p. 431.

35 Urwick and Wolf, op. cit., pp. 24-7.

36 Ibid., pp. 61-3.

37 Vangermeersch, Richard, "A Comment on Some Remarks by Historians of Cost Accounting on Engineering Contributions to the Subject," *The Accounting Historians Journal*, Spring, 1984, pp. 135-40.

38 Jelinek, op. cit., p. 85.

39 Church, "The Meaning of Scientific Management," op. cit., p. 97.

40 Ibid., pp. 98-9.

41 Church, "Intensive Production and the Foreman," op. cit., p. 830.

42 Merrill, op. cit., p. 211.

43 ASME, *Transactions: 1912*, p. 1142.

44 Ibid., p. 1156-9. 45 Ibid., p. 1204.

46 Church, *The Science and Practice of Management*, op. cit., iv.

47 Ibid.

48 Church, "Relation Between Production and Cost," July 29, 1915, op. cit., pp. 209-10.

49 Gantt, "Relation Between Production and Cost," August 26, 1915, op. cit., p. 385.

50 Ibid., p. 386.

51 Church, "Relation Between Production and Cost," Sept. 2, 1915, op. cit., p. 431.

52 Gantt, "Relation Between Production and Cost," October 21, 1915, op. cit., p. 737.

BIBLIOGRAPHY

Books

Alford, L. P. Editor, *Cost and Production Handbook*. New York: The Ronald Press. 1934.

———. *Laws of Management: Applied to Manufacturing*. New York: The Ronald Press Company. 1928.

American Society of Mechanical Engineers, The. *Transactions: Volume 34. Cleveland Meeting New York Meeting, 1912*. New York: ASME. 1913.

Brummet, R. Lee. *Overhead Costing: The Costing of Manufactured Products*. Ann Arbor: Bureau of Business Research. 1957.

Church, Alexander Hamilton. See Appendix A after Chapter 2.

Davis, Ralph Currier. *The Fundamentals of Top Management*. New York: Harper & Brothers, Publishers. 1951.

Ferguson, Eugene A. *Bibliography of the History of Technology*. Cambridge, Mass.: Society for the History of Technology. 1968.

Garner, S. Paul. *Evolution of Cost of Accounting to 1925*. Accounting History Classic Series. Original Edition. 1954. Reprint Edition. University, Alabama. The University of Alabama Press. 1976.

Jaffe, William J. *L. P. Alford and the Evolution of Modern Industrial Management*. New York: New York University Press. 1957.

James, Hurford. *Sons of the Forge: The Story of B. & S. Massey Limited 1861-1961*. London: Harley Publishing Co., LTD. 1961.

Lewis, J. Slater. *The Commercial Organization of Factories: A Handbook for the Use of Manufacturing Directors, Auditors, Engineers, Managers, Secretaries, Accountants Cashiers, Estimate Clerks, Prime Cost Clerks, Bookkeepers, Draughtsmen, Students, Pupils, etc.* London: E. R. N. Spon. 1896.

Makepiece, Chris, E. *Science and Technology in Manchester: Two Hundred Years of the Lit. and Phil.* Manchester: Manchester Literary & Philosophical Publications, Ltd. 1984.

Manchester Society of Chartered Accountants. *A Brief History of the Manchester Society of Chartered Accountants*. Manchester, England. Undated.

Margerison, Tom. *The Making of a Profession*. London: The Institute of Chartered Accountants in England and Wales. 1980.

Merrill, Harwood F. Editor. *Classics in Management*. New York. American Management Association. 1960. Renold Limited. Renold 100's 1879-1979. Manchester: Renold Ltd. 1979.

_____. *Sir Charles Renold J. P., L.D. 1883-1967 In Memorium*. Manchester: Renold Limited. 1967.

Solomons, David. Editor. *Studies in Cost Analysis*. 2nd. Edition. Homewood, Illinois: Richard D. Irwin, Inc. 1968.

The National Union Catalog: Pre 1956 Imprints. Vol. 108. London: Mansell. 1970.

Tripp, Basil H. *Renold Chains: A History of the Company and the Rise of the Precision Chain Industry 1879-1955*. London: George Allen & Unwin Ltd. 1955.

Urwick, Lyndall and Wolf, William B. *The Golden Book of Management: New Expanded Edition, in Two Parts*. New York: American Management Associations. 1984.

Wells, M. C. *A Bibliography of Cost Accounting: Parts I and II*. Monograph 10. Champaign-Urbana. Center for International Education and Research in Accounting. 1978.

_____. *Accounting for Common Costs*. Champaign-Urbana. Center of International Education and Research in Accounting. 1978.

Williamson, Harold F. *Winchester: The Gun That Won the West*. Washington, D. C.: Combat Forces Press. 1952.

Wren, Daniel A. *The Evolution of Management Thought*. New York: The Ronald Press Company. 1972.

Articles

Alford, L. P. Editor of *The Management Engineering*, in his note to Church's "Internal Transportation in a Large Textile Finishing Plant." April, 1922. pp. 197-202.

Calder, J. "The 'Principles of Management.'" *American Machinist*. June 13, 1912. pp. 965-6.

Cameron, A. T. "Review of Manufacturing Costs and Accounts." *Annals of the American Academy of Political and Social Science*, November, 1917. p. 294.

Church, Alexander Hamilton. See Appendix A after Chapter 2.

Coffman, Paul B. "Review of Manufacturing Costs and Accounts." *The Accounting Review*. April, 1930. pp. 85-6.

_____. "Review of Overhead Expenses." *The Accounting Review*. March, 1931. pp. 81-3.

Cole, William Morse. "The Interest on Investment in Equipment." *The Journal of Accountancy*. April, 1913. pp. 236-40.

Colley, F. G. "A Book Review of The Science and Practices of Management." *The Journal of Accountancy*, Dec., 1914. pp. 484-6.

Diemer, Hugo. "A Bibliography of Works Management." *The Engineering Magazine*. July 2, 1904. pp. 626-42.

Dunkerley, Roland, "A Historical Review of the Institute and the Profession." *The Cost Accountant*. September-November, 1946. pp. 12-20.

"Dunlap, John Robertson." *The National Cyclopaedia of American Biography*. Volume C. New York. James T. White & Company. 1930. pp. 434-5.

Editors. *The Engineering Magazine*. In a note preceding Church's "The Meaning of Scientific Management." April, 1911. pp. 97-101.

"First Award of the Institute Gold Medal: Presentation to Mr. Roland Dunkerley, JP, FCWA." *The Cost Accountant*. July, 1955. pp. 62-3.

Galloway, Lee. "Review of Production Factors in Cost Accounting and Works Management." *The Journal of Accountancy*. May, 1911. pp. 69-74.

Gantt, H. L. "The Relation Between Production and Costs." *American Machinist*. June 17, 1915. pp. 1055-6, 1061-2.

_____. "Relation Between Production and Cost." *American Machinist*. August 26, 1915. pp. 385-6.

_____. "Relation Between Production and Cost." *American Machinist*. October 21, 1915. p. 737.

Going, Charles Buxton. "Review of Manufacturing Costs and Accounts." *The Journal of American Society of Mechanical Engineers*. April, 1917. p. 369-70.

_____. "The Efficiency Movement: An Outline." *Transactions of the Efficiency Society*. Vol. 1. No. 1. 1912. pp. 11-20.

Greely, Harold Dudley. "Review of Manufacturing Costs and Accounts." *The Journal of Accountancy*. June, 1917. pp. 475-7.

H., F. A. "Cost and Time-Keeping Outfit of the Taylor System: Some Conveniences and Short Cuts of Obvious Utility." *American Machinist*. December 14, 1906. pp. 761-3.

"Index to the Periodical Literature of Industrial Engineering." *The Engineering Magazine*. July 2, 1904. pp. 643-58.

"Inspiring Growth of the New Science of Industrial Management." *Industrial Management: The Engineering Magazine*. November, 1916. pp. 145-8.

Jelinek, Mariann. "Toward Systematic Management: Alexander Hamilton Church." *Business History Review*. Spring, 1980. pp. 63-79.

Jenckes, J. M. "What a Foreman Should Know about Costs." *American Machinist*. November 11, 1915. p. 869.

Kimball, Dexter S. "Review of Manufacturing Costs and Accountants. *American Machinist*. March 8, 1917. p. 396.

_____. "The 'Principles of Management'." *American Machinist*. June 13, 1912. p. 965.

Lewis, J. Slater. "Works Management for Maximum Production." *The Engineering Magazine*. December, 1900. pp. 211-220.

Litterer, Joseph A. "Alexander Hamilton Church and the Development of Modern Management." *Business History Review*. Winter, 1961. pp. 211-25.

"Management." *American Machinist*. December 19, 1912. p. 1043.

McHenry, William E. M. "Relation Between Production and Cost." *American Machinist*. September 23, 1915. p. 564.

Mee, John F. "Pater Familae et Magister." *Academy of Management Journal*. March, 1965. pp. 14-23.

Miltimore, Louise S. "Introductory Note." *The Accountant's Index: 1921-23*. New York: American Institute of Accountants. 1924.

Morrison, C. J. "What a Foreman Should Know About Costs." *American Machinist*. October 28, 1915. p. 782.

"Obituary, Percy O. Lightbody." *Management Accounting (UK)* January, 1965. pp. 34-5.

Potter, R. R. "Review of Manufacturing Costs and Accounts. *Engineering News-Record*. April 19, 1917. p. 150.

Renold, Hans. "Engineering Workshop Organization." *Proceedings, Manchester Association of Engineers*. 1913-14. pp. 21-57.

Renold, Sir Charles. "Management Accounts." *The Cost Accountant*. September, 1950. pp. 108-28.

Richards, W. C. "Interest Not a Charge Against Costs." *The Journal of Accountancy*. April, 1913. pp. 240-1.

Smith, Gershom. "Distribution of Indirect Costs by the Machine-Hour Method." *The Engineering Magazine*. June, 1909. pp. 384-94.

Sterrett, J. E. "Interest Not a Part of the Cost of Production." *The Journal of Accountancy*. April, 1913. pp. 241-4.

"The Treatment of Interest on Manufacturing Investment." *The Journal of Accountancy*. April, 1913. pp. 231-44.

Thornton, Frank W. "Review of Overhead Expense." *The Journal of Accountancy*. August, 1930. pp. 150-1.

Vangermeersch, Richard. "A Comment on Some Remarks by Historians of Cost Accounting on Engineering Contributions to the Subject." *The Accounting Historians Journal*. Spring, 1984. pp. 135-40.

van Oss, A. "Review of Manufacturing Costs and Accounts." *The Journal of Accountancy*. July, 1929. pp. 72-3.

Other

Barnstead, Lloyd A. Personal correspondence dealing with Patterson, Teele & Dennis in New York. Mr. Barnstead was a partner in that firm. Letter dated July 10, 1984.

City Clerk. Taunton, Massachusetts. Personal conversation dealing with Alexander Hamilton Church.

Crum, Thomas L. Rector of St. Thomas Episcopal Church in Taunton, Massachusetts. Letter on December 31, 1982 concerning Alexander Hamilton Church.

Degan, Mr. Conversation with proprietor of Degan Funeral Home on December 29, 1982 concerning the burial of Alexander Hamilton Church.

"Diagram of Cost System: Revised Jan. 1908." Hans Renold Ltd. Copy of system designed by Church and Renold. This chart and many other artifacts of the days of Church at Renold found at the Archives of the Renold Company through the courtesy of its Archivist, Mr. Frank Crehan.

Gill, C. B. H. Telephone conversation in October, 1984 about the history of the firm, Parkenson, Mather & Co., in Manchester, England.

Jaffe, William J. Letter to writer about the life of L. P. Alford. Letter dated May 6, 1985.

Massey, Keppel. Letter to G. E. Royle, Commercial Manager, B. & S. Massey, Ltd., about the writer's inquiry about Alexander Hamilton Church. Letter dated April 5, 1984. Thanks to Geoff Royle for his help and kind hospitality.

Mee, John F. Various letters about Ralph C. Davis in the hopes of getting recollections about A. H. Church. No success could be achieved by the kind efforts of Mr. Mee.

Milliken, John. President of Mount Hope Finishing Company. Letter to writer in early 1983 concerning Alexander Hamilton Church.

Mortimer, Doreen L. Manger of Management Information Services of The Urwich Group. Various letters to the writer about the missing file Urwick had on A. H. Church. The file can not be located in Australia or in London.

Pell, Senator Claiborne (RI). Letter about research done on Alexander Hamilton Church by the Library of Congress staff. Letter dated December 11, 1984.

Probate Court Records for the estate of Alexander Hamilton Church. Taunton, Massachusetts.

Wellington. Roger. Former partner in Scovell. Wellington about the history of the company. Letter dated January 27, 1985.

Wells, M. C. Letter to writer on March 11, 1985 about A. H. Church and H. C. Alexander.

"Works Order and Sale Record" from B. & S. Massey files. Sample of cost system set-up by Alexander Hamilton Church. Courtesy of Geoff Royle.

INDEX